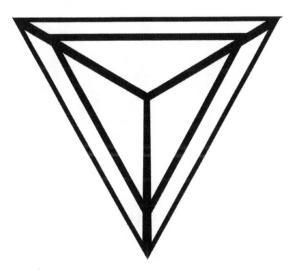

INDIRECT
WORK

InterOctave
14905 Bothell Everett Hwy Ste 362
Mill Creek, Washington 98012
www.interoctave.com

ISBN (paperback): 978-0-9893013-9-8
ISBN (ebook): 978-0-9893013-8-1

Ordering Information:
Special discounts are available on quantity purchases by corporations, associations, and others. For details, contact InterOctave at the address above.

CAROL SANFORD

WITH BEN HAGGARD

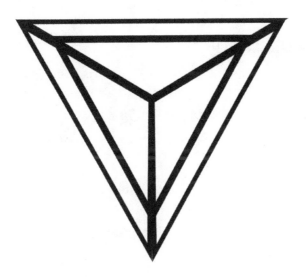

INDIRECT
WORK

A REGENERATIVE CHANGE THEORY
FOR BUSINESSES, COMMUNITIES,
INSTITUTIONS AND HUMANS

To Sylvia Packer, my granddaughter,
for bringing beauty and love into our lives.

CONTENTS

Foreword from the Boardroom

Ahmed Rahim, Co-Founder, Numi, OSC, and The Collective

Growing up, trying to integrate between two very different cultures—coming from the Cradle of Civilization, where a deep sense of belonging is instilled in everyone, to a culture where rugged individualism is most prized—I chose a professional journey as an artist and explorer of culture and community. I could not have predicted that someday I would become an entrepreneur, but once there, I had to learn quickly how to swim in the turbulent waters of commerce, competition, and finance. In time, having adopted the identity of CEO of a fast-growing business, my response was to do what I thought successful business leaders are supposed to do: set goals, be decisive, and drive results (measured chiefly in financial terms). While this approach seemed to work well by traditional measures, it didn't satisfy my ongoing search for deeper meaning.

For as long as I can remember, I've been curious to understand the why and the how, to discover the hidden layers in each experience, and to learn how to deepen my relationship with others and the larger world. But how this all worked together and how it could be applied to my everyday experience lived mostly in the realm of intuition; that is, until I had the chance to work with Carol Sanford.

By reading Carol's earlier books, *The Regenerative Business* and *The Regenerative Life*, and working with her personally, and by helping to launch several organizations (Numi, OSC, The Collective, Numi Foundation, and others), I've had the opportunity to stop and deeply reflect on patterns within myself and to heighten my state of awareness of what it means to be part of—and in service to—a regenerative living system. The lessons have been many, and they continue to unfold: how to get out of my own way by rewiring the thoughts and behaviors I've unconsciously adopted; how to move beyond a linear way of thinking and a desire for certainty toward embracing the present moment and recognizing the dynamic, systemic nature of life; and how to dissolve my awareness of self and recognize that, in everything I do, I am part of a collective, playing my unique role and helping to strengthen the greater whole.

Carol's lessons don't stop at ideas. She provides practical steps for tapping into one's purpose and living life as an extension of one's genuine essence. Over the years, as I put her guidance to work, I have shifted my approach to leadership, focusing more on building cultural values, asking questions with openness, advising rather than directing, collaborating, empowering others, creating a sense of belonging, and leaving doors open to creativity and magic. This has made a remarkable difference in the effectiveness and impact of the organizations I am privileged to steward and in the quality of life of those who are touched by them, including my own. Carol's insights and practices have also helped me shift my energy. I am more present in the moment, more trusting of the collective and accepting of the ups and downs that are part of the journey, and better able to stay connected to my essence.

Yet in the work of inner and outer transformation, it is hardest to know what you don't know, to see what you don't see. This is where *Indirect Work* comes in. In this latest book, Carol interweaves her teaching with artful intermezzos—exercises for activating one's inner reflections and creating new ways of thinking and approaching business, relationships, community, and society. It is an exploration, a journey that realizes the often-expressed principle that it's not the destination but how the journey is approached that matters. This is *the* critical work if we are to evolve our individual and organizational capacities to realize our highest purpose. It's the most exciting process to unravel, guided by pure openness to the present and to the greater collective.

When I reflect on Carol's total body of work, I see the vast ripples of change that have emanated from the wisdom of her teaching. She has a gift for shifting change-makers' consciousness and thinking, as she has shown with me and so many of my colleagues, moving us to adopt new ways of being in our work and give flight to bold solutions to the social and environmental imperatives of our time.

I hope this new book, along with all of Carol's teaching, will enhance your life as it has mine.

Foreword from Academia

Pamela J. Hinds, Fortinet Founders Chair and Professor, Management Science and Engineering, Stanford University

Indirect Work offers a radically different way to think about how to create change. It's clear to me, as it is to many, that we can't keep doing things the way we have. Even clearer, the methods that got us into our current ecological, social, and economic predicaments are not likely to get us out of them. *Indirect Work* presents a unique and powerful way to address the challenges of our time. It offers an in-depth introduction to Carol Sanford's theory of change, presented here in a compact form that is based on her decades of work as a highly successful educator serving businesses around the world.

This book is directed to change agents in all fields and at all levels, from students to seasoned professionals. The examples and stories are well-told, accessible, and moving, and they do a nice job of drawing readers in and helping them understand the points being made. Carol's overall message is clear and easy to follow from chapter to chapter. The intermezzos—pauses interspersed among the more theoretical chapters—are fabulously effective. They invited me to reflect on my own experience as a way of engaging more deeply with the material. By giving me real work to do, the intermezzos encouraged me to integrate what Carol has to say about bringing change to the world and apply it to the issues that drive me.

At a higher level, *Indirect Work* challenges our existing paradigms and theories of change and provides a well-reasoned, documented alternative. We can't bring about sweeping transformations in our practices and systems by taking them on directly as big problems to solve, as we do now. *Indirect Work* proposes instead that we make fundamental changes in ourselves and come to know our places as effective agents in ascending orders of living systems. In other words, it helps readers know *how* to "be the change you wish to see in the world." Don't try to tackle what seems most wrong out there; develop the unique potential within yourself and then, through indirect work and in everything you do, be a resource to others and help them to see theirs. This is an iterative process and both an age-old and a brand-new way of bringing about transformation.

In this sense, *Indirect Work* is a wildly hopeful book. Anyone can read it and get value from it. Based on my own experience, it seems to me that whoever takes time to read the chapters carefully and work through the intermezzos will immediately make changes in the way they're engaging with issues, and these will inevitably lead to beneficial effects in the world.

I have known and worked with Carol for almost 30 years. What I've learned from her has had a big influence on the way I think about the communities and endeavors I am a part of, my role in the world, and what it means to have impact. We have always agreed that our own ongoing learning and development are necessary to the ways that we engage in the world. This is core to the message of *Indirect Work*—that by helping others develop their own capability, we help to create the conditions for transformative and lasting change in the spheres to which each of them will dedicate their work.

Carol's focus on capability building, the core activity in the stories and primary component of indirect work, seemed especially apt to me in my role as teacher. When I work with students at Stanford and elsewhere, I structure my teaching in ways that include exploration and reliance on lived experience, moment to moment. This encourages my students to find their own meanings in what they are learning. Their agency is strengthened, they become *capable* learners with the ability to develop as *capable* professionals, and they confirm or begin to know the roles they want to take on in their lives and careers.

I love this latest addition to Carol's publications, and I look forward to reading it again. It articulates some important aspects of the work I do and illuminates how it is possible for me and others to make real change happen in the world, as individuals and as members of communities and society. The ideas in *Indirect Work* have triggered in me a profound realization of the importance of working in community and holding in awareness the communities that we affect beyond our own—recognizing effects rippling out from individual and collective contributions. It leaves me with a powerful, enduring, and visceral sense of the incredible possibilities alive in my connections to things larger than myself.

Introduction

Making My Escape

In the summer of 1964, straight out of my junior year at a Baptist college in Abilene, I hit the road with a carful of fellow students determined to see the world. It was my first time away from Texas, and although I didn't realize it, I was engineering my escape from an abusive childhood and a narrow religious culture that had no use for independent, outspoken women. Our little band of renegades followed the fabled Route 66 to California, driving for three days and sleeping on the ground at roadside parks in the time-honored tradition of college students everywhere. By the time we washed up in Hollywood at the home of my roommate's uncle, I knew I was never going back. Nine weeks later, I had met and married the man with whom I would have two children. Soon after, we moved to Berkeley, where he would pursue a master's degree and I could pick up where I left off as an undergraduate.

It was a tumultuous time at UC Berkeley, with the rise of the free speech and antiwar movements. I found my interests evolving as I moved from a focus on political science to political philosophy. This led me to a survey course on Greek philosophy, where my first encounter with Plato's Socratic dialogues and the "allegory of the cave" rocked my world. It was so obvious: in that mad ride from West Texas to California, I had escaped from the cave. My eyes had been opened to a bigger reality than I had ever imagined possible in my sheltered Christian upbringing. Reading the dialogues awakened in me a fervent desire to become a philosopher and to support others who, like me, were seeking meaning in their lives.

The allegory of the cave, which lies at the heart of Plato's *Republic*, is one of the fundamental images of Western thought and culture. In the dialogue, Socrates describes a cave in which people are chained in place, unable to move, watching flickering shadows on the wall that they take to be reality. (This image is the basis for the popular movie *The Matrix*, which also shows human beings enslaved and pacified by an illusionary reality.) For one who has been freed from the chains, it becomes apparent that the shadows are produced by puppeteers holding up cutouts in front of a flickering fire. It takes a philosopher, a lover of wisdom and seeker of truth, to endure the painful process of climbing out of the comforting darkness of the cave to stand in the light of the sun.

Over the years, I've applied this image to my work in the world, which has focused on evolving the underlying beliefs and premises that organize human activity on our planet. Most of this work has been in the field of business and organizational development, although some of it has spilled over into the fields of governance and social change. For me, the shadows represent the world as it is conveyed to us by our senses, and the chains are the paradigms and mental models by which we interpret this world. The puppeteers are the priestly caste of experts and opinion leaders to whom we look in order to learn what is true, right, and good. The fire that casts the shadows is the cultural milieu that shapes what we believe, know, and consider worthy of knowing.

It takes deep and diligent work to see the hidden machineries (the puppets and puppeteers, chains and shadows) that generate consensus reality. Helping others to see these machineries is even harder because they believe the puppet show. It's not enough to tell them they are caught in a shadow play. To free them from the cave, one must build the capability and consciousness that will enable them to examine the hidden sources of their perceptions of reality. One must grow a culture and community of fellow seekers, each aiming to break the mechanical patterns of their thought. This is what I mean by *indirect work*.

A philosopher doesn't try to persuade us that this or that phenomenon is a shadow on a cave wall. Instead, she provides us with the method and means to step out of the cave and its illusions so that we can see for ourselves. We do this by learning to challenge the apparent evidence of our senses and the interpretations we make of this evidence. Indirect work teaches us to discern and then evolve the reality-making apparatus within ourselves.

Indirect Work is intended to serve as a key to my other writings, in particular my books and blog posts.[1] I have long understood that my words and teachings are often misinterpreted because people try to understand them as direct instruction. They want a template, something they can apply directly, something they can do. But what I'm saying has to be approached from the vantage of an indirect mindset. Otherwise, everything that I'm describing is downgraded to tactics rather than experienced as an invitation to examine the source of one's beliefs about reality.

I hope with this book to evoke a shift in perspective that will enable readers to perceive the world in a new way. I sincerely believe that we will not make the urgent changes needed with regard to all aspects of how we live if we don't learn to work indirectly. I've even built in a set of exercises, presented here as brief intermezzos, to support this shift. I encourage you to use this text to challenge and explore your own processes of reading and making meaning.

---

1 Carol Sanford is the author of five previous books: *The Responsible Business: Reimagining Sustainability and Success*; *The Responsible Entrepreneur: Four Game-Changing Archetypes for Founders, Leaders, and Impact Investors*; *The Regenerative Business: Redesign Work, Cultivate Human Potential, Achieve Extraordinary Outcomes*; *No More Feedback: Cultivate Consciousness at Work*; and *The Regenerative Life: Transform Any Organization, Our Society, and Your Destiny*. She blogs at carolsanford.com.

Chapter One

A New Map

Once upon a time, I used to take client groups I was working with to visit projects that I had helped establish. I wanted to inspire them and give them a sense of what was possible. Then one day I realized that what I was doing was having the exact opposite of its intended effect. When I walked onto the project sites, I could see all kinds of things that were invisible to my tour participants. I could see people thinking creatively on their feet, open to new insights and information unfolding in present time. I could see processes and product offerings that were systemic enough in their implications to transform industries. I could see managers and workers interacting nonhierarchically, aiming toward shared purposes. All of this was visible to me because of the new mind I was using to interpret the phenomena in front of me, but it was always mostly invisible to the people on my tours, who were working from their old minds, chained in Socrates's cave. What they saw simply served to reinforce what they already "knew" to be true.

I believe that this self-reinforcing pattern of thought is the crucial issue of our moment. Most of us agree that things need to change, that neither society nor our planet can maintain their integrity if we continue on our current path. But confusion arises when we try to figure out what change actually means and how to make it happen.

Many people believe that change means reshaping our practices, improving what we do and how we do it. I call this *working directly*, as if we were all billiard balls on a vast table. If we exert the right force in the right direction, we can knock everyone into the ideal positions to function harmoniously and sustainably. This forms the basis for the majority of theories of change operating in the world today.

For me, these approaches to change are all working from an old mind. We've modified what we do, but we haven't addressed who we are. It's no accident that nearly every philosophical and spiritual wisdom tradition teaches that profound and enduring change can only come from transforming who we are and how we experience and understand the world. This is indirect work, an instrument with the potential to change the world when it is understood within a framework for a coherent theory of change.

Albert Einstein, in his characteristically pithy and quotable way, once said that "you can't use an old map to explore a new world." Yet even with the best intentions, this is what most of us do most of the time. As I write this text, aimed at challenging the habits of outmoded and comfortable ways of thinking, I know that readers will be using these same ways of thinking to navigate and understand it.

I want to invite you to set aside the old map, to allow the language in this book to construct a new one in its place. It's so much easier said than done, but here's a simple practice for you to consider. Whenever what I've written here *seems* to confirm what you already believe and to fit with your current way of working, pause and ask yourself what you are missing: "What is being said here that really *doesn't* fit? What requires me to change who I am and how I think?" Even if the words I've written fall short of perfectly articulating this different mind, I believe that, through our joint effort, you can challenge your own certainties in order to make space for a new way of seeing the world. You will not be aiming for a static template or model; you will be enlarging your capacity to observe and evolve your own thinking and your potential to create change.

INTERMEZZOS

To support this joint effort, I've interwoven my chapters of narrative with a series of intermezzos, offering exercises for resourcing your reflection. These are designed to help you notice the presence of the old map and begin to describe for yourself the features of the new one. I know that it will be tempting to skip these exercises and read straight through the book to see what the lady has to say. The problem with this is that, although you may be entertained by what I have to say, you won't necessarily learn anything new about yourself and how you think. Therefore, to get the most out of your reading, I encourage you to use the intermezzos as a way to come into dialogue with your experience of the text.

The deeper purpose of the intermezzos is to develop your capability to manage, filter, process, and discover ideas as they arrive in your mental space. This requires *intentional self-observing*, the creation of *a conscious awareness, separate from ongoing mental activity, that allows one to objectively observe this activity*. It is a common spiritual or consciousness-development practice, and in some traditions, it is referred to as cultivating an "inner witness."

Once this witness is present, it becomes possible to really notice how we take in influences from others, whether we are reading their words, listening to them speak, or absorbing what they are modeling through their behavior. Learning is at least as much about how one engages with new information and experience as it is about the information itself. The extent to which a person can manage their own mental state will have a decisive influence on what they are able to receive. Some states allow us to see and be affected by something new, whereas others filter and reinterpret what we're seeing so that it fits within our preexisting categories and assumptions. Some open us to surprising new depths of understanding, while others sweep out the jewels because they seem to have no value. I suspect that we've all had this experience in our lives, when we couldn't receive a teaching because we weren't ready. The purpose of self-observing is to create greater likelihood that we'll be ready and won't toss out the teaching because of old, ingrained habits of thought.

Working with Intermezzos

You will encounter eight of these intermezzos as you read through the book. They will invite you to pause, reflect, and do a bit of journal writing in response to a set of questions. The intention is to evoke self-observing and self-discovery in relation to what you've been reading. In my experience, this builds capability to choose how your mind is working and at what level rather than hum along on autopilot.

As you read, pay particular attention to how your preexisting ideas shape what you think I'm saying. Let your normal process of reading take hold, but at the same time, be aware of it. Notice if you are renaming or restating the ideas and concepts that I've offered in order to make them more familiar. Or notice if you find yourself reshaping their meanings because you find my meanings too obscure. See if you can catch yourself feeling aligned with what I'm saying rather than challenged by it—this is often an indicator of filtering out what's genuinely new in a concept and thereby losing its value.

If you do catch yourself doing any of these things, make some journal notes. This can be a very powerful way to reinforce your self-observing and your ability to gain more from what you're learning. You can also make notes about how you might be able to use what you're reading. This puts you into the experience and helps make the ideas more concrete.

Finally, *allow the intermezzos to interrupt you and even to disrupt you.* Stop and answer the reflection questions. Do the creative exercises before reading on. This will help you receive much more from the book than you would if you read it without them. Who knows? They might even change the way you read other books and listen to other speakers, and that could open your mind and transform your life!

First Intermezzo

Begin by getting yourself a journal in which to work on all eight of the intermezzos. I recommend that you handwrite your entries rather than creating a digital journal, because there is real benefit in engaging the body in the process. Using a pen or pencil helps build connections between the two hemispheres of the brain and enhances the wholeness of your cognitive experience. Or, if handwriting is a burden, rough out your work on paper and then work it again in an electronic file. Don't seek perfection. Instead, allow yourself to go deeper and see further. *Messy* is a perfectly acceptable look for learning, good thinking, and creating.

For your first journal entry,

- Write out, in short form, the top five things that you believe about how to make a better world. In other words, as a well-intentioned person, what do you think helps to create the change you want to see? Here are some examples that come out of my interactions with people: "Always start with people where they are." "It's all about building relationships." "We all need to commit to a lighter footprint on Earth." "We have to eliminate hierarchies (or capitalism or consumerism or racism or sexism or heterosexism or gasoline engines and plastic, *etcetera*)." Try not to borrow from my examples. See if you can get to the core of your own beliefs about what will create the changes needed for lasting transformation.

- Next, for each belief, make a list of practices that you use to put them into action. Over time, as you think of other practices that are informed by these beliefs, you can add them to your list.

- Reflect on the pool table metaphor for direct work in the context of your own work. Notice any relationship between the metaphor and your actions.

As you read each of the following chapters, make a note in your journal whenever an idea really catches your attention. Make some notes about what attracted you to it and what, if anything, it leads you to want to do. *Do this writing before you read the intermezzo following the chapter*, which will include reflection on both your notes here in this first exercise and your notes for the chapter.

And finally, hold in mind the simple exercise I suggested earlier. Whenever what I've written *seems* to confirm what you already strongly believe and to fit with your current way of working, pause and ask yourself what you are missing: "What is being said here that really *doesn't* fit? What requires me to change who I am and how I think?" Reflecting in writing on these questions should provide plenty of grist for your mill as you make your way through all of the chapters.

Chapter Two

A Story Of Change

In the early 1980s, the Chicago Bulls were a lackluster team on a long losing streak. Then, in 1985, something changed. They began to win game after game, setting new records and introducing radical new plays and strategies. This shift in fortune coincided with an infusion of new talent, especially the recruitment of a young Michael Jordan onto the team. But this kind of turnaround depended on more than just hiring the right group of players. It wouldn't have been possible without the behind-the-scenes influence of someone who eventually came to be seen as the greatest coach that basketball has ever known.

Even as an assistant, Phil Jackson was already developing a philosophy of coaching that was indirect and very effective. It emphasized team culture, collective will, and shared intelligence rather than the mechanics of basketball. It also emphasized the deeper meaning and value of the sport and the spiritual development of the players as a way to find and express this meaning.[2]

Faced with Jordan's extraordinary talent, Jackson knew that he would have to evolve the ways he thought about coaching. Jordan was an individualist, a star accustomed to carrying teams on the strength of his own skills. Before joining the Bulls as an assistant coach, Jackson had himself been a professional player, which shaped his belief that basketball is fundamentally a collaborative activity and defi-

---

2   For more on Phil Jackson's life and coaching philosophy, I refer readers to his own books on the subject, *Sacred Hoops: Spiritual Lessons of a Hardwood Warrior* and *Eleven Rings: The Soul of Success*.

nitely not, in its essence, simply a showcase for stars. With the Chicago Bulls, he would need to find a way to transform a group of aggressively competitive egos into a unified mind.

His efforts in this regard were supported by deep dives into Zen Buddhism, yogic meditation, and study with Lakota elders. In contrast to Jackson's Pentecostal upbringing, each of these practices emphasized the importance of finding one's own answers to life's questions through profound inner development. From this perspective, basketball is a way to foster the unique spirit of players, not a way to extract cash value and entertainment from their prodigious skills. Growing the spirit and capability of great players in the context of team play is the most powerful way to create the conditions for great basketball.

Jackson developed players by helping them to develop consciousness of the interdependence of individual and team. He taught them to observe their breath as a simple way to manage their mental and emotional states, using it to calm and focus their energies even under intense pressure. He also used breathing to unite the team, teaching a practice that he called "one breath, one mind," in which players breathe together, listening to one another until the breath becomes one. This allowed each player to expand his awareness in order to take in the whole team, experiencing it as a single, unified organism or phenomenon.

Jackson also dimmed ceiling lights during practice sessions, forcing players to use all of their senses and capacity for perceptual awareness to keep track of the whole of what was happening on the court. Through these and other experiences, he was able to build a sense of unity in the team until they knew in their bones that it wasn't an individual who scored a point but the whole team working together. Players developed compassion for one another and for the members of teams they played against. They learned to think together in motion and to see the game as a highly dynamic system whose properties were revealing themselves in real time. This enabled them to move beyond rote moves to invent new forms of play, live and in the moment.

But perhaps the most significant change Jackson introduced was his insistence that players had a sacred duty to the sport and to its fans. The game, he reminded them, was about spirit, not about scoring. As high-profile celebrities, they were role models, and it mattered what they did on and off the court. When they played beautifully, both in physical and spiritual terms, then the whole world benefited. By carrying themselves with dignity and compassion for one another, their competitors, and their fans, they helped shine a light on what it could mean to be human.

Jackson reinforced this culture of conscious caring through his own behaviors. He didn't critique his players, telling them that what they were doing was wrong or boneheaded. Instead, he asked them to reflect for themselves, as individuals and as a group, on how they had played and how well they had managed their states of being. He invited them to consider the effects of their choices, not only on the basketball court, but in all their professional activities and every aspect of their personal behavior. Later, many of his players reported that this man had helped change their lives, their families, and their commitment to service in the world.

(The story has an interesting coda. When he left the Bulls after 13 years, Jackson went on to lead the LA Lakers to extraordinary success, helping shape the careers of Kobe Bryant, Shaquille O'Neal, and others. Meanwhile, his replacement at the Bulls reverted to a more conventional coaching style, drilling the team on plays, haranguing them to play better, and emphasizing the importance of winning. Needless to say, that was the end of the Bulls' long run as champions.)

Working Indirectly

I tell this evocative story—and I will continue to elaborate upon it throughout this book—because it illustrates the point I am making. Profound change rarely comes from direct interventions in the world. Rather, it comes from working indirectly over time, helping people engage consciously to develop their own understanding, motivations, aspirations, and will. All sorts of human endeavors can benefit from this approach. I have used a sports example because sport is widely familiar; its dramas unfold before our eyes on courts and fields and in gymnasiums; and it's clearly archetypal.

Like everyone else in the sports world, Phil Jackson understood that the industry of professional basketball is geared toward winning games, attracting spectators, and generating lots of money. He knew to his core that helping (or even driving) his players to deliver on these outcomes would corrode their characters and weaken or possibly destroy the team's cohesiveness. Conventional values of the profession encourage players to adopt a star mentality, jockeying for position and time on the court and in front of the cameras in order to advance their own careers and incomes. Unfortunately, this self-serving orientation undermines the performance of a team and decreases the likelihood that it will achieve the kind of success that owners seek.

Jackson's way out of this dilemma was to place his attention, and the attention of his players, on the larger meaning of what they were doing. Basketball, he believed, is an honorable, even a sacred, pursuit. It can build aspiration and character in those who play it and express beauty, camaraderie, and spirit to those who watch it. He built champion teams not by working directly on their skills or income-generating capacity, but by building their passionate dedication to playing the game with honesty, respect, fairness, cooperation, and conscious engagement. He didn't train vicious competitors; he cultivated role models, and in the process, he elevated the value and attractiveness of the entire sport.

Along with this orientation to the larger meaning and potential of basketball, he also placed strong emphasis on building self-determination in his players, enabling them to make quick, intelligent decisions in the heat of a game. This is the opposite of conditioning, which trains players to repeat a specific pattern, often without a lot of conscious involvement. Unfortunately, conditioning has become the norm in our society, not only in sports, but in industry and education. It is a toxic artifact of behaviorism, which was introduced in the early 1900s and dominated thinking about human management for much of the last century.

Jackson was a very effective change agent, working at multiple levels. His players credit him with helping them to transform themselves, giving them an experience of collective purpose and discipline that enabled them to pursue lives of service after the ends of their careers on the court. These personal transformations drove what they were able to accomplish by working together as real teams, seamless and highly intelligent wholes, to deliver record-breaking results. Jackson's work ennobled the game, and it demonstrated the effectiveness of conscious human development as a powerful engine for innovation and excellence.

Jackson is celebrated for what his teams were able to do under his guidance. People are fascinated and curious about how he did it. But very few leaders have taken his approach to heart. His results are obvious, but his means are indirect and seem obscure, and this is often too challenging a way of working for leaders who are trapped in the old paradigm. Bridging the gaps in understanding that arise whenever the old paradigm is confronted by the new requires at least a minimum of personal, and sometimes professional, reorientation.

The Story's Deeper Message

I believe that many people, perhaps most people, seek to lead moral lives. That is, to the best of their abilities, they seek to do what is right and good in order to have a beneficial effect in the world. At the same time, I believe that it is no accident that people fail over and over again to produce these intended effects. In their efforts to do good, they are unintentionally keeping in place the very infrastructures (mental and physical) that they would like to transform.

Well-intentioned people, businesses, and organizations everywhere suffer from this dilemma. Even as they promote their achievements to their customers, stakeholders, and the world at large, they recognize that things around them are not really changing. This, they assume, is because not enough people are doing what *they* are doing, and so they advocate more strongly for their approach. It doesn't occur to them that their approach might be precisely what is creating the ceiling that they are bumping up against and, because they are the ones we look to as leaders of social change, that we are all bumping up against together.

What they can't see is that their thinking and actions are based on an outdated and discredited understanding of how the universe works, a condition they share with most of us. Collectively, we are trapped in a mechanistic (or even more archaic) paradigm, and this causes us to make seemingly logical and ethical choices that actually produce destructive results. The urgent question now is how to provide leadership that is more appropriate to the world we find ourselves in, a world that is in crisis precisely because of the paradigms from which we've been operating.

We look to the moral and honorable people among us for leadership. We recognize their agency, that they have willingly taken up responsibility as stewards for the world they find themselves in. But they are hindered in their ability to do this work by a failure to understand living processes and the ways change happens in human systems. Unfortunately, because they are honorable in their intentions, it can be very hard for them and for us to see that they are a large part of the problem. Yet any time we operate from a mechanistic paradigm—when, for example, we create programs and certifications and ideal solutions to take to scale—we reinforce the underlying patterns that are the source of the problems we wish to solve.

I hold a premise that *all* human beings share responsibility for making this shift in how they see the world, whether or not they have awakened to it. Our work as a species is to be conscious participants in and stewards of life's evolutionary processes. To do so will require far more from us than simply to repair the damage we've done to the world and to one another, and it will require more than becoming better people. It also requires us to examine and make discernments about how we think, how we make sense of things, and how we shape our actions accordingly. We must undertake to do this ongoingly, bringing it into every aspect of our lives and institutions, because it's a capacity that needs to be built and evolved. Without this most fundamental change in ourselves, we can't bring about the change we seek in the world.

SECOND INTERMEZZO

First, review your notes on the Chicago Bulls' story and its message. What were you able to observe about your own filters? How is your mind working to interpret what you're reading?

Over many years of working on myself and with other people, I've developed some premises about what's required to be able to *observe the working of one's mind while engaged with some activity*, such as reading this book. In my experience, bringing attention to the question of how we filter new information is a good start, and this is what I asked you to do as you read each chapter. However, simply paying attention is not enough because our interpretation of what we are observing is still continually shaped by old patterns, beliefs, and biases.

These intermezzos are not about interpreting or making meaning of my words and ideas or discussing how they affect you or how you might apply them. Avoid the practice of using an author's ideas as a stimulus or starting point for a train of thought. Instead, watch your inner process, and while you are reading, ask yourself, "How am I reading and how is it affecting my interpretation of the text? What am I projecting onto the text that isn't really there? How am I letting myself get in my own way as I try to hear the author out?"

We need a way to rigorously examine our own thoughts and those of other people, and that is the role of the frameworks I use to disrupt the models implicit in old ways of thinking. Here is a framework that I believe can help you become more rigorous as you investigate your engagement with information and how you take it in:

LEVELS OF WORLDVIEW

LIVING SYSTEMS

HUMANIST

AUTHORITY

Authority. At this level, we look to someone else to provide the right thoughts for us or to confirm the thoughts that we have. Instead of anchoring our thinking in our own experience and the development of our own reasoning and discernment, we give this authority to others. Once upon a time, superior knowledge would have been expected to come from the king or the church. Now, it's more likely to come from experts and opinion makers. In Western cultures, this worldview is common in childrearing, education, government, and business. The effect is a constant erosion of creativity, responsibility, and agency in citizens and organizations alike.

Humanist. At this higher level, we believe in the potential goodness in all things and work hard to nurture this goodness in our children, relationships, and environment. Our first premises are that human nature and the world are perfectible, and it is the responsibility of humans to promote this perfection. The humanist approach is strongly characterized by the pursuit of ideals and the desire to share these ideals.

Many of the readers of this book have been influenced by the humanist view and are actively seeking to make the world a better place. The easy-to-miss downside of all these good intentions is that they are fundamentally anthropocentric. In the humanist view, humans are agents who act *upon* the world rather than a single species among millions of others that dwell *within* the world, a dissociation that causes us to imagine that change is accomplished by our direct work. If I (the *subject* of my heroic narrative) can amass enough resources, information, and power, then I can push society or nature (the *object* of my intentions) to rearrange itself.

Living Systems. Here at the level of living systems (which includes most Indigenous and some Asian worldviews), we start from the assumption that all living beings have their own agency and purpose. There is no need to impose our will or our ideas of what they should be; instead, our work is to cultivate the humility and receptivity that allows us to understand what they are striving to become. From this understanding, we begin to discover appropriate roles for ourselves within their processes of becoming. Our work shifts to evolving the infrastructures and instruments that will enable them to develop for themselves the capabilities they will need to make their own contributions to some other entity's becoming. Those of us who aspire to play this role must engage in our own development, taking back our projections onto others and turning what had been outer work into inner work.

You can see the three worldviews in the trajectory of Phil Jackson's personal story. He was raised in an extremely authoritarian church and no doubt experienced plenty of authoritarian coaching when he was a professional basketball player. Early on, he was drawn to the humanist approach of Tex Winter, who had developed methods for getting basketball players to work collaboratively, as teams, rather than pursuing their own self-interests. But the real breakthroughs came when he figured out how to apply the living systems worldview he had internalized through his exposure to Lakota and Buddhist teachers. At this point, he developed truly indirect ways of working, providing the players he coached with the means to make their own connection to the spirit in the game and in themselves.

The Levels of Worldview framework provides the underlying structure for examining your thinking process as you read all of the following chapters. Returning now to your journal, make some notes about your answers to the following questions. And, as you do so, imagine me sitting with you as a friend, asking them as a way to help you get more of what you were looking for when you picked up this book.

- Reflect on the list you made in the first intermezzo of the top five things you believe will make a better world. In each case, do you know where you got the idea? Can you guess which worldview informs it?

- Next, have a look at your journal notes about ideas that excited you, or if you didn't jot anything down, look back at the introduction and first two chapters for reminders. As you continue developing the ability to assess your thoughts using the levels of worldview, can you catch yourself having reinterpreted a living systems idea at a humanist or authority level? As you notice any reinterpretations, make some notes about your reflections on your own reading process.

- If you were to give yourself instructions for how best to read the next chapters of the book, what might these instructions be?

- Now, go back to your reading and enjoy! Remember to make journal notes whenever you are attracted to an idea and *whenever you catch yourself reinterpreting something in the text*. Also remember to apply the instructions for reading you've given yourself. In your notes, describe any difference you notice them making.

Chapter Three

A Theory Of Change

I confess to being a lifelong rabble-rouser. Although I had a strict Evangelical upbringing, I learned from a young age to question the world around me. This was partly due to the influence of my Native American grandfather, who quietly encouraged me to know my own mind and to think about my place and my responsibility in the cosmos. By the time I was a junior at a conservative Christian college in Texas, I was being thrown out of Bible class for questioning the need for women to subject themselves to the wills of their husbands.

But it was at UC Berkeley that I finally experienced a true shattering of my certainties. I was auditing a series of guest lectures by the philosopher of science Thomas Kuhn, who introduced us to the idea that the paradigms by which we understand the universe can and do evolve. I was thunderstruck. I had already gone through my own profound evolution of paradigm—from a belief in the literal truth of the Bible to a belief in the literal truth of science. Here was a thinker challenging me to recognize that the new ground I was standing on was no more permanent than the old. I needed to learn to pay attention to the working of my own mind and the way it used paradigms to make sense of my experience.

Moving Beyond Certainty

For the next 15 years, I pursued the implications of this insight. I noticed that the evolution of paradigms within a culture wasn't a linear process. I could see that old paradigms were still very much alive in institutions and people around me and that many social conflicts could be seen as conflicts of paradigm. I witnessed different paradigms fighting it out inside my own mind. This led me to observe that paradigms had distinct qualities or patterns. I could see that my mind, when it was operating with a mechanistic view of the world, was very different from my mind when it was seeing the world as alive and whole. You could say that they were *entirely different* minds. It was becoming clear to me that it mattered which mind I was using because these differences impacted the quality and creativity of my thinking. Eventually I concluded that paradigms were best understood as a hierarchy, with each new evolution opening up a new order of understanding about the nature of reality and our relationship to it. This led me to create, along with Charlie Krone and other colleagues, a theory of change based on a paradigm of a living, evolving universe.

A FOURFOLD PATH

My approach to working on change is grounded in the concept of *hidden variables*, a term that comes from pioneering quantum physicist and philosopher David Bohm. Bohm, who was described by Albert Einstein as both his protégé and his colleague, had an insight early in his career: certain seemingly inexplicable phenomena could be mathematically explained if you allowed for influences that could not be directly perceived or measured.

Bohm called these influences "hidden variables" and quickly came to realize that they applied to more than the problems encountered at the level of subatomic particles. Many of the conflicts between physics and philosophy, human behavior and spirituality, and quantitative and qualitative ways of understanding the world could be reconciled through the concept of hidden variables. Bohm offered a theoretical foundation for a radically different way of thinking about reality and change, and this foundation was embraced and honored by his friend Einstein.

A regenerative approach to change can be understood as a confluence of four hidden aspects of what we often refer to as "reality." Each of these has the effect of shifting our attention away from direct, material interventions and results and onto the invisible patterns that lie behind them. This is an example of bringing to the foreground what had formerly been background.

The first of these aspects I call *matrix*, to refer to the womblike, interwoven substrate that nourishes and enables life to exist. I selected this term not only for its original meaning but also because of popular associations with the movie of the same name. In the film *The Matrix*, consensus reality turns out to be a very persuasive illusion overlaid on a deeper truth. To make real change, one must act indirectly on these deeper levels rather than directly on the illusion.

The second aspect I call *the way*. This focuses attention on the fact that it doesn't matter how good or virtuous the subject of our work is if we approach it from the same old fragmenting (and therefore life-denying) approach. You have to start with the right mind, which means starting with the right paradigm or reality base. Once you are grounded in a living systems reality, you make different choices, not only about the way you work but also about what you choose to work on.

The third aspect I call *implicate order*, a term that also comes from David Bohm. Bohm offered a useful language for thinking about three dimensions of reality: apparent, hidden, and cosmological. He described these as three interdependent orders for understanding and interpreting the universe—the explicate, the implicate, and the supra-implicate. The explicate order addresses material existence, which we can perceive with our senses and our instruments. The supra-implicate order addresses cosmological questions having to do with why humans exist. The implicate order addresses the invisible dynamics (including hidden variables) that pattern what gets brought into existence, dynamics that we can learn to understand even though we can't perceive them directly.

The fourth aspect—which I have already told you a little about and which is the primary subject of this book—is *indirect work*. In a nutshell, indirect work has to do with awakening the inherent human tendency to want to develop and evolve, especially when we feel connected to a larger sense of purpose and meaning. This desire becomes a far more effective engine of change than any autocratic impulse, no matter how benevolent, to control and direct human actions and choices.

Together these aspects can be understood as a dynamic tetrad, a framework, useful for understanding the ways in which they relate to form a cohesive theory of change, with high potential for conceiving of and transforming the world as a living whole.

A REGENERATIVE THEORY OF CHANGE

Implicate Order

Matrix   *The Way*

Indirect Work

Matrix sits at the ground point of our framework, which means it is the right starting point if we want to discover and express the highest possible level of potential in this particular inquiry. Matrix is the nurturing context that enables things to develop, just as the womb provides the conditions of shelter and nurturance for the baby developing within. The quality of the context is a limiting condition for the quality of potential that is available. If the matrix is vibrant and healthy, the thing we are trying to develop has far more likelihood of success.

Every living being—including complex entities like organizations, communities, and ecosystems—is embedded in a larger context from which it derives nourishment and a sense of meaning. The idea of matrix reminds us to look beyond a specific subject of interest in order to take into account the systemic processes that affect it. Unless we attend to these larger processes, it isn't possible to ensure the full and healthy development of the beings we care about. In fact, we are likely to undermine their health and integrity if we fail to give full consideration to the effects of these systemic influences.

For example, what a pregnant mother eats affects her gestation process. Sophisticated farmers tend the life and health of their soil as a way to ensure excellent crops. Head Start programs, which emphasize play, inspiration, and socialization, are far more effective at nurturing children's reading skills than tutoring programs with a narrow focus on reading. And so on—we can see the truth of this claim everywhere we look.

In his work with basketball teams, Phil Jackson introduced practices that helped his players reconnect to the matrix on demand, when needed. Traditionally, most coaches have worked on training, putting players into simulations of the game, drilling them in order to habituate specific skills and reflexes. Jackson worked on developing capacity for remaining conscious of the whole. He taught his players to meditate and to breathe together, so that whenever they were on the court, they knew how to remain connected to one another and to everything that was happening. He was famous for gathering a team together in the fever pitch of a game to invoke the collective mantra, "One breath, one mind." At the moments when things were most likely to fly apart, he helped players learn to regain connection. "Keep your eye on the spirit, not the scoreboard," he reminded them. In this way they grew the capacity to be in the game while remaining above it, and thereby able to manage its complexity and dynamism.

In application, working on matrix means developing an understanding of the context within which activities take place. Through intelligent interventions in the context, we can greatly enhance the effectiveness of our activities. For example, it's much more effective to manage clean water by maintaining the health of upstream forests than by building purification plants, and an upstream forest also provides habitat and flood control.

In work settings, if you are trying to grow the capacity for teams to work more effectively, it's important that you focus on much more than the specific activities and output of their work. You also have to take into account the way they are thinking about their work and awaken their aspiration to help one another pay attention to their thinking. This implies that they have a shared sense of where they could be going and who they could become as a team, if only they could improve the quality and the results of their efforts.

The way, or the goal point on our framework, describes the source of meaning and significance that keeps us moving forward with an activity, even when the going gets tough. The way is not a destination but the uprightness and integrity with which we walk the path that we are on. This inner integrity, accompanied by the continuous learning and development that come from being on a path, is a very powerful but hidden variable when it comes to change.

This lesson is hidden in plain sight in Phil Jackson's story. He was working with professional players, highly competitive individuals who lived and breathed basketball. If he could help them connect their love of the game to a desire to more fully and beautifully express their potential, then they would become unbeatable as a team. If, on the other hand, he connected their passion to a narrow purpose like winning or becoming famous, it would drive them toward mediocrity. His work was to open up for them the sheer joy of being present in the moment, working harmoniously together to collectively express all that was possible in that moment, for themselves, the competing team, and the witnesses in the stands.

Most of us are familiar with setting and pursuing goals and the motivation they can provide. But not all goals demand the development of character. This was the situation that Phil Jackson encountered in the world of basketball, where character-corrupting goals like fame, wealth, and winning were common. By lifting up goals that had more meaning and significance built into them, he awakened in his players a respect and desire for inner development. "Millions of kids are watching you to see how a hero behaves," he reminded them. "How do you need to live and play to be worthy of their admiration?"

This was second nature to Jackson, who had stepped onto the path of Buddhism as a young man, as well as having taken instruction from native elders in the Way of the Lakota. His challenge was to bring these ideas to his players so that the quality of their being and bearing became more important to them than the trappings of celebrity. From his own experience, he knew that the way was not something you could dictate to people. It wasn't a list of appropriate behaviors and attitudes to be reinforced by carrots and sticks. It was an inner light that could be awakened in each player, invisible to the eye but shining through their lives.

I describe the path that he was inviting his players onto in terms of three interrelated disciplines: developing *capability*, creating *culture*, and evolving *consciousness*. By working on these disciplines, Jackson knew that his players and his teams would naturally evolve who they could be in the world, and that this shift in being would have profound effects on how they performed—in life and on the court.

With regard to *capabilities*, I see two critical things that Jackson was working on. Inwardly he was helping players learn to manage themselves and their states so that they could remain calm, open, imperturbable, and fully awake—even in high-pressure or provocative situations on and off the court. In practices, Jackson would explicitly create situations that were unfair in order to enable players to face their *emotional* game.

At the same time, he was helping them develop their critical thinking so that they could make systemically intelligent and appropriate choices in the heat of the moment. He built team strategy around the triangle offense developed by Tex Winter, which required players to invent offensive and defensive moves, minute to minute, based on maintaining a coherent pattern of relationships throughout a game. He also avoided calling timeouts during play because the development of the team's thinking in crisis was paramount.

Obviously, these two capabilities of self-management and critical thinking are closely related. It's nearly impossible to engage critical thinking when one's state has collapsed into distraction, anger, or fear. The meditation, breathing, and awareness practices that Jackson introduced helped players remain calm and self-possessed even as they extended strategic awareness and connection to everything that was happening around them.

Capability development was supported by a strong team *culture* that emphasized mutual endeavor and the subordination of personal ego to a shared purpose. "One breath, one mind" was more than a centering practice for individual players. It also created the conditions that allowed the team to operate as a unified being, with a collective intelligence that far surpassed the talents of any one player. In the same way, the triangle offense distributed play across the whole team, requiring that players work together while reducing the desirability of becoming a star and the opportunities for doing so. Within a field of mutual support, it was natural for players to develop their individual capabilities quite rapidly.

The most elusive but powerful discipline had to do with the evolution of *consciousness*. Capability and culture, although vitally important, are limited in their effectiveness without the ordering influence of consciousness. Consciousness provides the context and orientation toward which our awareness, self-management, and collective work are directed, and it depends on being able to discern different levels operating within phenomena. For example, Jackson wanted his players to have a deep understanding that basketball was not just what happened on the court. It was also an industry that affected the lives of fans and promoters, host cities, and thousands of people who depended on the team for their livelihoods. Beyond that, it was symbolically significant in the life of the nation, and the way players and the team as a whole approached it could have a positive or negative influence on that national identity. Perhaps most important, sport needed to be embraced as a spiritual path that fed players' souls because otherwise the industry would eat them alive.

Basketball is all of these levels at once, but it takes effort to maintain consciousness of the multidimensionality of the game. Jackson sought to help his players gain capacity for this kind of consciousness because, as long as their attention was limited to what happened on the court, they couldn't spiritualize the game.

They had to be able to move up levels of significance, recognizing that the transformation within themselves was key to enabling basketball to transform the lives of fans, cities, and nations. By recognizing and imbuing the game with its true power and potential, they could place their extraordinary talents in service to something deeply meaningful and develop the spiritual dimension of their humanity in the process.

Implicate order, the direction point in our change theory framework, offers the guiding principle that allows us to grow the integrity of our work in service to evolving systems. In this case, I've adopted David Bohm's concept of *implicate order* as the source of a particular state of mind that allows us to experience life and the universe as whole and undivided.

Bohm developed this concept because the laws of classical physics were inadequate to describe or explain the phenomena observed by Einstein and the pioneers of quantum physics. Classical physics, locked into the dogma of cause and effect, wasn't equipped to understand the kind of noncausal behaviors revealed in the laboratories of these scientists.

In a major insight, Bohm realized that this was a failure of outmoded concepts, a failure, if you will, of the core axioms on which Western science has been based since the time of Aristotle. He recognized that what was needed was a new way of observing and thinking about phenomena based on understanding the universe as fundamentally whole, undivided, dynamic, and indeterminate. He called this mental perspective the "implicate order" and articulated it through a set of theorems that served as alternatives to the laws of classical physics.

Once we begin to pay attention to the way that the old, classical physics informs our thinking and the thinking of the people and institutions around us, we begin to recognize that it's ubiquitous. For example, every time we try to solve a problem, dividing it into its components to understand it better, seeking to figure out its causes in order to address them, we fall under the spell of classical mechanics. Every time we translate something into a replicable (and therefore scalable) procedure or recipe, we've stepped into a machine universe. This is so pervasive in Western and now global culture that it becomes invisible to us. It can be very difficult to get our minds to shake off this continually reinforced pattern in order to question our fundamental shared beliefs about how the universe works. But this is exactly what Bohm, in his pioneering investigations into a quantum universe, asked us to do—build an entirely new basis for thinking.

Although he was raised with a perfectly conventional American education, Phil Jackson's early exposure to Lakota and Buddhist ways of thinking and being gave him access to a non-Western view of life. Artificial distinctions between humans and nature, mind and body, doing and being, individual and context, were challenged or even dissolved within these Indigenous and Eastern worldviews. I believe that operating from the implicate order became second nature to Jackson, so much so that it was difficult for him to shape his choices and actions from a classical Western perspective. At times, this put him in conflict with his employers. But it opened up enormous potential for his players.

For example, Jackson knew from his own experience as a highly competitive college and professional basketball player that, whenever a coach told him what to do, he would resist. Even if he didn't argue with them out loud, he would certainly argue with them in his head. In other words, he had enough self-awareness to recognize that he had become fragmented and polarized in his thinking. He was no longer a whole person within the whole of the game and the whole of the cosmos.

In his career as a coach, he conscientiously avoided such polarizing attempts to exercise control over players, seeking instead to harmonize their distinctive talents, ambitions, and intelligences within a larger shared purpose. He was very careful to cultivate shared systemic understanding and clear personal agency.

The key to making this possible, to enabling the team to lift itself up out of the explicate and see the implicate order of potential, was to cultivate the capacity for reflection. Players needed to learn how to observe themselves in order to break old patterns of thought and behavior, and this wasn't easy because the allure of the familiar always tends to drive the mind back into its ruts. To establish new patterns, Jackson would challenge them again and again, and they would challenge one another, to assess themselves in relation to an agreed-upon framework.

Through education and self-evaluation, players came to understand the *system* of play that they were using (including its principles and strategies). Jackson would literally put it up on the board each time they met in the locker room, a place away from the heat of the moment on the court, where extended reflection was actually possible. In this way he created a ritual reminder of the systemic consciousness they were all working to develop and gave authority back to players as the captains of their own development.

Players also looked within themselves to discover the roles that each could play within this system. In this way, they took on responsibility for using the system and living up to its potential, and they did this as part of an explicit, collective agreement. If Jackson asked them to do something, it was always framed within the context of this agreement rather than as him pulling rank. On the occasions when he took players to task, it was to disrupt them from destructive patterns in order to remind them of the system.

This ubiquitous mental orientation toward wholes may explain why so few coaches have followed in Jackson's footsteps. It's not enough to copy his practices or his approach. After all, his approach was arising in the moment in response to the needs of his players and of the game. (This, by the way, is exactly why best practices don't work.) The underlying source of the inspired uniqueness of his ideas and ways of working was his experience of the world and the unconventional thinking processes that this enabled. In order to understand his story, we need to recognize that we are encountering someone who sees, thinks, and engages from the implicate order, a completely different way of understanding the world than the ones we are accustomed to. This is the source of his sustained success in achieving a "miraculous" winning streak.

Indirect work, the instrument at the bottom of our framework, refers to the real-world means for going to work on everything I've described above. I call it *indirect* in order to emphasize that this approach is never about forcing things to happen, controlling outcomes, telling people what to do, or supplying the answers to their questions. Rather, *indirect work is building the capacity in people to consistently think at higher levels in order to create innovations for advancing specific contexts and streams of activity.* This capacity allows us to become instruments for the regeneration and evolution of the living systems within which we are nested— to become effective change agents.

Because indirect work is our primary interest here, I am now going to pause and offer an intermezzo and then move on to a discussion of the *technology of change,* the practical work we do to develop the capability, culture, and consciousness characteristic of the way.

Third Intermezzo

I'm guessing that as you read chapter 3 you were able to be more observant of your process than you had been when reading the earlier chapters. I know that when I do this exercise, I get better as I go along. In my experience, the ability to remain intentional and self-observing while acting or working is an important (and hard) part of being conscious. Let me offer a few more questions for your journal to help you keep improving. It's ironic that we humans are perfectly capable of developing our self-observing capacity, but we're almost never taught how.

- So, what worked this time that you weren't able to do as you read the previous chapters? How did you catch yourself? What changed, as you worked with the instruction that you gave yourself?

- What did you learn about yourself from watching these patterns? In particular, did you notice a tendency to drop back into the chapter's content and out of observation of how you were engaging with it? Were you able to observe less of how my content affected you and more of how your inner processing affected your reading of it? Are you feeling upset? Do you notice that you have attachments that color or cause you to reject aspects of my presentation, my examples, or the story I'm telling? How are the contents of your mind and your habits of thinking affecting your engagement with the book?

- As you read the Bulls' story, did you find yourself hoping that Jackson would make more direct interventions for specific *better* outcomes? Where did you project yourself into the story, imagining how your ideas and ways of working would produce better results than Jackson's?

- What gift did you just give yourself by observing your own reading process?

- Can you see ways to improve your instruction to yourself as you set out to read the next chapter? While this is fresh in your mind, try it out with at least the first section.

Chapter Four

A TECHNOLOGY OF CHANGE

I'll start here with an analogy I sometimes use to make the idea of indirect work more immediate. Over the years, I've noticed that we often act as though life is a game of pool and people around us are cue balls. Our job is to nudge them with the right amount of force in the right direction to knock the rest of the balls on the table into the pockets that we've designated for them. But people aren't cue balls. They are living beings with almost unlimited potential for self-direction, creative action, and conscious development.

Even more important: in our dynamic, whole universe, human consciousness is one expression of the tendency or potentiality of the living systems that we are embedded in. That is, our ability to engage the world consciously is not the activity of fragmented or isolated human individuals; it is a property of the living matrix of the world that produced us. This means that, just as it is inappropriate to treat human beings as cue balls, it is also inappropriate to objectify and manipulate any living system, any aspect of life, as if it were on a pool table. We are not on Earth to knock things around.

This realization is at the core of David Bohm's response to the atomization that resulted from classical physics. When we are able to fully internalize his insights into explicate and implicate orders, we begin to experience everything in our world in new ways (or actually in ancient ways, from the perspectives of many Indigenous peoples). In real-world terms, what does it mean to work on change in an indirect way, translating the emerging science and philosophy of living wholes into practice? As has always been the case, this translation is made by creating a technology: in this case, a technology for the development of the latent capacities of human beings, consistent with a living paradigm.

I propose a technology of indirect work built around developing the triad of disciplines that describes the way, or the goal point on our change framework: capability, culture, and consciousness.

THE WAY TRIAD

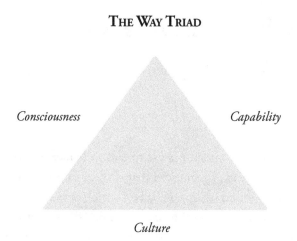

Consciousness   Capability

Culture

A new paradigm, informing a different way of experiencing and working in the world, will require the development of different capabilities than most of us have now. These capabilities are difficult to acquire or sustain outside of a community and culture within which mutual support and learning can occur. The trick is to build or evolve culture at a level that doesn't simply reproduce old patterns of thought, and this requires the development of consciousness.

Consciousness, in this context, refers to the ability to recognize different levels or orders of world. In other words, it takes consciousness to shift from an explicate to an implicate view of reality. Consciousness informs a developmental culture, which supports the growth of new capabilities, which then become the occasion for seeking new consciousness. These three disciplines are *essentially* interdependent and synergistic.

A Regenerative Epistemology

I want to take a brief detour into the subject of epistemology, the philosophical term for theories of how humans know what we know or how we learn. I am introducing a technology of change that is different from everything that is commonly practiced in organizational, political, or educational arenas because it works on inner development as a means to outer transformation. This technology is based not only on a theory of change but also on a distinctive epistemology that gives it power and effectiveness. Without some understanding of inner development based on this regenerative theory of knowing, it is extremely difficult to apply the technology change in a way that maintains its integrity, and this can lead to unsatisfactory or even harmful results.

I start from the premise that there are different natures of knowing and that some are of higher quality than others. One level of knowing is focused on what I call *borrowed ideas*, the stuff I take in from media and experts, and even what I've learned from people I deeply respect. What characterizes borrowed ideas is that they come from outside of me and I accept or reject them uncritically, usually because I have some reason to trust or distrust their source. An epistemology of borrowed ideas is all about knowledge transfer. It assumes that, for you to know what I know, all I need to do is tell you, by giving a lecture, writing a book, or doing a media interview.

Another level of knowing focuses on *analyzed ideas*, those that I've looked at critically, testing them against my experience and the accumulated expertise of humanity in order to decide whether to accept or reject them. What characterizes analyzed ideas is that they have stood up to my own scrutiny and been judged worthy. This means that I have some kind of model to test them with, or that they've been thoroughly debated, or that I've tried them out myself in practice. An epistemology of analyzed ideas is all about learning the criteria for sound, critical judgment, so that I can have confidence that what I know is actually valid and worth knowing.

Deep understanding, a third level of knowing, is the focus of my epistemology. It starts from the premise that ideas or information lack meaning and power until we subject them to the inner work of understanding. That is, I might know a great deal about a subject or a person and still not actually understand them. This epistemology uses the instruments of reflection, introspection, and imaging to gain and grow understanding through time.

Why is this important? The regenerative theory of change that I am introducing here is grounded in the inward move from knowledge to understanding. To understand anything requires an inner shift, a willingness to immerse ourselves in experience, allowing whatever we are studying to fully enter our awareness, become illuminated by reflection, and thereby change us. Without this willingness, all of the best ideas in the world, let alone in this book, remain inert—just more grist for the mill of a mechanistic mind. The stories I've chosen to tell here can be taken in as knowledge—Phil Jackson did this, that, and the other with his team, and that's why the Bulls won a championship and why we should do what Jackson did. But this would completely miss the point. Phil Jackson did what he did because he understood the basketball players he was working with, understood their situations, understood the game, and understood how to work indirectly on manifesting what it was capable of becoming.

A Technology of Change

It is fairly easy to see a coherent technology for human development, informed by an epistemology for self-developed, deep understanding, behind the way Phil Jackson worked. At the level of capability, he sought to grow the ability of his players to manage themselves—to exercise the power of their own minds to be imperturbable in the face of chaos or stress and to understand the systemic effects that flowed from each action they took, whether on the court or off. With regard to consciousness, he helped each player build a bridge to the meaning of basketball as sport, a sacred trust rather than a physical activity.

Jackson also fostered a culture of selflessness, a term that he uses often to describe the spiritual potentiality embedded in the game. Toward this end, he offered a system, Tex Winter's triangle offense, that each player committed to of their own free will. One of the cornerstones of this system was a set of principles for how a winning team plays. On one level, these principles were technical descriptions for how to deploy a team on the court. But, at a deeper level, they reflected a systemic philosophy that emphasized the intelligent working of the team as a whole.

For example, players learned to overcome the unconscious tendency to focus on and move toward the ball. Instead, they learned to maintain consciousness of the whole court, the even distribution of the team across the court, and the distinctive skills of each member of the team. As they became proficient, every team member was able to see and play the whole of the game and, in their individual contributions to the action, to utilize the whole of the team. Every player was thinking as coach and master strategist. These thinking capabilities demonstrate what I mean by exercising the power of mind; they are also what created in the Bulls a bond of unity born of selfless dedication to the success of the whole.

Jackson was drawing on more than just smart basketball as he worked with this system. He later reported that he could see a mirror of what he had learned from the Lakota in what Tex Winter had designed. As a university student and star basketball player, he got to know a group of young Lakota men who were living at his grandfather's North Dakota boarding house. They asked him to teach them basketball, and before long he was coaching them on a regular basis. It soon became clear to him that he was learning as much from them about life and working as a team as they were from him about the game. This experience made such an impression on him that he went on to study with Lakota elders, who taught him something important about the training of young warriors: the freedom of the warrior is a freedom *for* the tribe, not a freedom *from* restrictions. In other words, we gain true freedom when we set down ego and enter into selfless relationship with a community.

As I mentioned above, technology is the means by which we translate science and philosophy into practical application. Although in the present day the word has come to be strongly associated with machines, especially those that manage information, virtually every human endeavor is associated with a technology. In the case of human development, the currently dominant technology has been informed by the philosophy and science of behaviorism, which bases the management of human motivation on a mechanistic model of punishment, reward, and feedback. This model made a certain kind of sense within an industrial system that viewed workers as interchangeable parts in the machineries of production. It was also deeply dehumanizing, based on the idea that people were most effectively managed and manipulated by external means, as if they were rats in a lab or balls on a pool table.

The technology that I am introducing here is based on the idea that internal motivation and self-management are far more powerful sources of creativity and coherence than any system of external motivation could ever be. My philosophical starting point is that every person, without exception, has inherent capacities whose lack of development creates an artificial ceiling to their potential. The opportunities to develop these capacities are almost completely missing in our society, given its mechanistic bias, yet they could be built into everything from parenting to education to business to governmental programs. This is exactly why my colleagues and I have dedicated our lives to evolving a developmental technology.

What makes the Chicago Bulls' story both touching and brilliant is Phil Jackson's recognition of the need for and his constant striving and experimentation to create such a technology. He was able to prove again and again that the development of players' capacities could blow the lid off their ability to perform, and that this went far beyond what they could do with a basketball. Through his commitment, Jackson demonstrated the recognition of and care for his players as whole, multidimensional human beings rather than as one-dimensional prodigies. He also demonstrated dedication to evolving a better game and, by extension, a better society.

The Way

Taken together, work on capability, culture, and consciousness comprises the indirect method needed to recognize the hidden variables at play in events. The fact that these are *three* core ideas isn't an accident. More than 40 years ago, I had a fundamental insight about what it would take to address the conflicts and issues facing the world. This came out of a fertile period in my life when I was interacting with people who were reflecting on and applying philosophical and spiritual ways of knowing to transforming global businesses in order to reshape their impacts on society and the planet.

I could see that nearly all of the world's conflicts grew out of a binary or polarized view of reality: good/evil, right/left, male/female, White/Black, profit/loss, owner/worker, wealth/poverty, future/past, energy/matter, ones/zeros. Business, politics, psychology, and even religion were all busy trying to shift things from one column to the other within a zero-sum universe where one person's gain was inevitably another's loss. Or, when they weren't seeking to win the game, they were seeking to maintain its equilibrium through careful compromises and the balancing of powers—complementarity rather than polarity.

Faced with the ubiquity of this way of thinking, I realized that the way out of its dead ends had to do with the power of three-ness in a two-force world. In my flash of insight, genuine creativity came from not accepting the rules of win and lose. Rather, one had to see the dynamic tensions between opposing forces as the *sources* of evolutionary energy. This required stepping outside of the polarity in order to recognize its potential within a larger context. Stepping outside introduced a new, third force, one that was not bound by the terms of the conflict but could embrace both sides (or multiple sides, for that matter) as contributors to a new possibility.

This shift of levels from two to three forces is quite evident in the Bulls' story. As Jackson directed his players' attention away from winning and losing and onto the larger cultural meanings of basketball, he also helped them move their attention off the ball and onto the whole system of the game. This freed players and opened up a uniquely creative space within which they could invent new plays in present time and in response to all of the interacting dynamics of court and arena. Players learned to maintain consciousness of the whole of the situation, with its many layers and complexities, and this allowed them to escape the mechanics of the game and experience themselves as agents within a living phenomenon.

In my own case, this insight opened the way to a lifetime of experimentation with increasingly complex systems. I've developed extensive capacity for generating and working with multidimensional frameworks as a way to evolve my thinking. But all of this work has been based on that first liberating realization that if I could step out of a polarized dynamic and view the situation from a different level and scale of system, then unlimited potential could be opened up.

The three terms of the way offer the same kind of opening. Working on them has the effect of moving us into a dynamic and evolving relationship to life, one another, and the universe. Let's explore them separately for the purpose of understanding their dynamism as a whole, starting with capability and moving to culture and consciousness in chapters 5, 6, and 7.

FOURTH INTERMEZZO

You might have noticed that the intermezzos are providing exercises for developing the capability to read mindfully. For me, mindful reading has always been fun, and it has supported my ability to think independently. I'd like you to share this experience and reap the full benefit of reading this book, and so I dare to ask, *Are you actually doing these exercises, or are you just reading them?* Let's make this question the basis for our next set of reflections:

- Do you notice a tendency to resist the exercises? To skip over them? Why? Where does this resistance—this belief that "these exercises are kind of fun, but they don't really apply to me"—come from?

- If I've planted a seed of the idea that there's more than one way to read a book, how can I engage your curiosity about what it takes to change your own reading process? What would you need to say to yourself to persuade you to give it a try? Or, if you've been doing the exercises, to invest a little more deeply?

- We've looked at resistance, and we've looked at curiosity. Assuming you still want to play, give yourself a new instruction for how you want to read going forward. Distilling from what you might have done in the earlier exercises, pull up from your intuition or pull out of your thoughts a phrase that's really energizing. Write it in your journal. You can use it as a reminder or mantra for mindful reading as you proceed with the next section.

CHAPTER FIVE

CAPABILITY

Capability is what enables us to function effectively in the world. Becoming capable is not necessarily the same thing as acquiring knowledge or skill, because people can be highly knowledgeable and skillful without being particularly effective (a distinction that serves as a common trope in sitcoms and other comedies). Capability has much more to do with managing oneself and one's environment in order to apply knowledge and skills toward the creation of a desired effect.

This implies that capability has to do with *order* and *freedom*. Bringing order to our thinking gives us the ability to make sense of the information around us by relating diverse impressions within a coherent and whole understanding. Well-ordered thinking in turn provides the basis for appropriate action, freeing us from confusion and fragmentation and enabling us to make insightful and creative choices. Order, in other words, is the necessary partner to freedom, and capability embraces them both.

THE CAPABILITY FRAMEWORK

This first point on the Way Triad can itself be understood as a three-term framework. Specifically, the capabilities that I believe are central to the development of human capacity are *imperturbability* and *working backward from effects*, fueled by *exponential powers of understanding*.

The Capability Framework

Exponential Powers of Understanding

Imperturbability

Working Backwards from Effects

Exponential powers of understanding is a term that refers to a basic capability of the human mind, which is to function at more than one level. The kind of mental activity needed to carry out routine activities is quite different from what's needed for problem solving, creative innovation, or profound insight. Each of these requires different investments of time and mental energy, as well as different qualities of understanding. I find that the easiest way to describe these differences is by use of a metaphor of *levels*, as though there were multiple minds operating one above another. As one moves up levels, the available power of mental activity increases exponentially.

Thing Mind – One level of mind engages directly with the world of things, experiencing objects and events as discrete and fragmented. This can be useful for dealing with the automatic activities we're faced with in day-to-day life, such as getting the clothes washed, roof fixed, and kids to school on time.

Process Mind – At the next level, we see existence in terms of process, dynamism, and flow. This way of understanding the world around us more accurately reflects the continual change characteristic of everyone's experience of life. We adapt and learn from rapid change and develop new skills within evolving conditions. But although a process orientation is a far more sophisticated way of understanding existence than orientation to things, it doesn't naturally lead us to think about potential, or what could exist. This limits our ability to go beyond responding to conditions to transforming them.

Essence Mind – Transformational work occurs at another level up and is inherently a creative process. It brings into existence something that hasn't existed before but is present in the form of innate potential. To access this potential, we engage with living entities—from organisms to communities to ecosystems to processes—as they seek to more completely express their essences into the world.

Sourcing Mind – Finally, at a fourth level, is the mind that can evolve itself by observing the fundamental principles that inform how it interprets the world and then testing and developing them. This is the mind that is able to inquire into the implicate sources of evolution itself. It generates frameworks by observing itself at work and extracting an underlying principle.

Let's make these levels of mind a little more concrete by applying them to an old proverb. The *thing* mind solves the problem of hunger by giving a starving person a fish. The *process* mind teaches the starving person to catch a fish for herself. The *essence* mind explores the specific experience of fishing: "Who is this person I'm hoping to help? What is the nature of her place, its water, the fish it produces, its people and economies? What is the effect that all of this has on me? What is my essence and how do I bring it into harmony with the essence of this person and place? And what, ultimately, does this tell me about fishing, hunger, ecosystems, and economies?" The *sourcing* mind dismantles the proverb, questioning the fundamental premises or beliefs from which it was created and seeking the insight needed to move beyond it.

Phil Jackson was clearly teaching basketball players to move above the first two levels in order to see the essence patterns and potential unfolding in multiple dimensions in every moment of every game. I've always been particularly interested in the source of Jackson's innovations—how he was able to penetrate deep into the potential of basketball in America. I believe that it came from his desire to live what the philosopher Socrates called an examined life. In spite (or perhaps because) of a strict Pentecostal upbringing, Jackson learned to question his own thinking and beliefs, challenge his own certainties, and embrace not knowing as a necessary antecedent to creation.

This is a perfect example of the sourcing mind at work. Although I've seen no evidence that Jackson was explicitly seeking to teach deep self-inquiry to his players, I'm guessing that the transparent way in which he lived it may have opened a door for some of them. On the other hand, later in life, through his writings and his work with business executives, he has overtly attempted to communicate the underlying source of his effectiveness. Creativity was continuously available to him because of the level of mentation he was able to access. Unfortunately, although this is easy enough to say, it's almost impossible to fully convey in writing (a difficulty that also applies to this book).

Imperturbability is related to disruption—we wouldn't need to be imperturbable if we never encountered major upsets in our lives and work. In general, we humans dislike challenges to our routines, habits, and assumptions, and will go to great lengths to prevent having our lives turned upside down. But attempting to prevent disruption is quite different from being able to embrace it and work with the uncertainty it brings. The ability to maintain one's center and agency in difficult or even chaotic circumstances is valuable not only for individuals but for societies and organizations.

Imperturbability requires cultivation and yields significant rewards. It is a good example of a capability that works indirectly, by fostering stability of one's being state even in destabilized situations. This is why it's fundamental to everything from Phil Jackson's work with his teams to Buddhist and other mindfulness practices. In high-stakes settings, such as companies and governments, it can make the difference between reactive decisions and thoughtful, strategic choices. This is why I have made the development of people's ability to manage their inner states a central aspect of my work on organizational change.

Working backward from effects enables us to put new powers of understanding and imperturbability to work. We learn to choose our actions based on the systemic effects we hope to produce, given our current level of understanding. This assumes an ability to generate mental images of complex systems at work as a basis for forecasting because, in our living universe, relationships between actions and effects are indirect and complex. Working backward from effects also assumes the ability to reflect and refine one's understanding of systems dynamics in order to create increasingly effective future interventions. Without this mental capability, careless or thoughtless actions can easily lead to unintended destructive consequences, regardless of how high-minded our intentions might be. To understand how this works, it's helpful to begin by distinguishing among results, outcomes, and effects.

Results are the direct product of an action—they can be measured. For example, I recently bought a new computer that is intuitive to use and comes with quick and effective customer support whenever I run into difficulties. This enables me to write and do research with a level of ease and technical support that would have been unimaginable when I was a young graduate student. As a result, I am a happy customer and will buy from this company again in the future.

THE
Power *of* Thinking

POWER IS UPSTREAM

HOW
We Think
(Frameworks & mind at work)

WHAT
We Think
i.e. Subjects

THINKING
OR "Thoughting"

ACTION

Performance
/Results

Outcomes

Systemic EFFECTS

Outcomes are indirect, or secondary, products of an action that develop over time; they can be correlated but not necessarily measured. In the case of my new computer, the outcome is an experience of creative freedom, discovery, and expression. It has opened up new possibilities for building credibility and a platform from which to exercise influence with regard to the things I care about and aspire to change in the world.

Effects are truly indirect products of an action—they show up as systemic changes and will be invisible to anyone who hasn't developed the capacity to look for them. In my case, the freedom to grow myself as a writer has produced real, systemic effects in the world, effects that go far beyond anything I would have been able to do directly. Business owners and leaders from many nations have taken up the call to become agents of transformation through changing the ways they work with employees, suppliers, and customers. Students of regenerative thinking have drawn on the work I've published to help shape a dialogue about the fundamental ways we need to evolve our thinking in order to address multiple global crises. Notice that these effects have no direct relationship to my computer and only an indirect relationship to me. Yet they are produced by the action of the personal computer revolution in my life and the way that this has enabled me to make a creative contribution.

Effects, in other words, are elusive. They are the *indirect* products of action; the ability to discern them requires the sourcing mind because it is capable of producing an equally indirect and powerful understanding. In practical terms, this means identifying the right order of effect to be pursuing and then closely examining the beliefs and assumptions behind the choices we make about how to pursue it. Both sides of this equation require that we be able to observe and evolve the sourcing of our thinking.

Let's first look at what I mean by right order of effect. When thinking about this in the context of some improvement we wish to make in the world, the discipline is to use the sourcing mind to see what is behind this desire. Most of us start at the level of results—"I want to take this action because I expect it to produce that result"—and thus we need to drive our thinking back to where this wish was sourced. What do we actually care about, and what is its essence? This line of inquiry eventually delivers what I call a *global imperative*, a compelling description of how something works when it is in integrity with its own potential, such that one feels called to help it manifest this integrity.

Having established what is truly imperative, one can then ask, "How do I create the conditions that will produce this effect? What sorts of action will I need to take in order to create these conditions?" The primary purpose of this book on indirect action is to encourage and support readers' self-examination by introducing the thought that indirect actions might be orders of magnitude more effective than direct ones when it comes to pursuing their global imperatives. This is where it is necessary to examine one's assumptions about what constitutes an effective action.

As Phil Jackson evolved his thinking and practice, he slowly came to realize that he wasn't working on basketball; he was working on creating a healthy society. In particular, he was working on society's need to develop the capacity for consciousness and selflessness in young men—a function that in many preindustrial societies was accomplished through rites of passage. He has written extensively about how he had to overcome his own tendency to correct his players, to work directly on their posture, performance, or attitudes. He came to see that *mindfulness* was key to developing their full potential, and with this realization he was able to generate a radically new approach to coaching.

FREEDOM AND ORDER

Exponential powers of understanding, imperturbability, and working backward from effects are capabilities that embrace both freedom and order. I hope that my descriptions have made evident the kind of inner freedom that they can produce. Order shows up the minute one commits to developing them, making them the foreground of one's efforts, and putting them to use in the world. As a general rule, we bring order to what we do through the infrastructures we build to support it. What, then, is the kind of infrastructure needed for the development of human capacity?

Phil Jackson has written about the difficulty he faced in helping Michael Jordan integrate himself into the evolving culture of the Bulls. The infrastructure that has built up around the game of basketball rewards personal accomplishment within a ranking system that produces social and economic benefits for individual players (magazine covers, product sponsorship, *etcetera*). This has the unintended consequence of discouraging team effort. As a natural prodigy, Jordan had a hard time getting his head around the idea that he should sacrifice his own opportunities to score in order to increase the likelihood of building a championship team. To address this, Jackson recruited him as an ally in the team-building effort, which worked, in part, because Jordan's mother had encouraged him as he was growing up to look out for other kids in the neighborhood.

Together, Jackson and Jordan invested themselves in creating an alternative infrastructure. It may be great to encourage players to share the ball more, but the structure provided by the triangle offense enabled them to do this in a way that won games. It's great to introduce practices like meditation and using the breath to come together, but ritualizing them as a part of daily or weekly training provided the structure that made it possible for individual players to fully internalize these practices. This internalization was key to realizing the full potential of the triangle offense.

Altogether, these shifts enabled the team to become the most glamorous superstar, more than any individual player. Fans found Bulls games exciting because they could never predict who would score. Opponents were challenged to create a defense that addressed the whole team, not just Jordan, which made for even greater excitement. And although his individual scoring might have been somewhat diminished in a given game, Jordan's talents were set off by the innovative teamwork within which they were expressed. In the long run, this actually burnished his reputation, fame, and earning potential—and opened the way for other Bulls players to acquire some of the magic.

Destructive infrastructures—infrastructures that prevent or restrict the development of human capacity—can be seen everywhere, not just in basketball. For example, educational systems rank children as gifted, average, or special-needs students, depending on how well they conform to a generic set of expectations. This ranking determines the types of programs they will have access to and the nature of investment they are deemed worthy of—distinctions that become even more exaggerated in low-income communities. By design, these systems ignore children's inherent and differentiated potential as members of a learning community (or learning team—the analogy with basketball is exact), and it puts them in competition with one another for attention and accolades. This creates a star system that has lifelong consequences, more likely to be devastating than beneficial.

The same patterns of ranking and exclusion can be observed in businesses, governmental programs, and general social dynamics (for example, the perceived differences between "good" and "bad" neighborhoods). This raises the question of how we will create infrastructures in all of our institutions that foster the development of the capabilities I've described. How do we generate insights comparable to those that enabled Phil Jackson to turn the profession of basketball coaching on its head? From my perspective, developing answers to these questions will be fundamental to creating the kind of change that I believe we are seeking here, together.

FIFTH INTERMEZZO

These intermezzos are taking on some of the quality of ritual as they periodically interrupt your ordinary way of engaging with a text and invite you to reflect and reconnect with your original purpose for reading this book. By now, you may have noticed that these rituals are adding value that you wouldn't otherwise have gotten. The first three questions below are intended to make this value explicit:

- How does this ritual disrupt existing automatic patterns and open up the possibility of new ones?

- What's shifting in your ability to watch yourself as you engage in these patterns? Why is this potentially useful?

- What have you gotten from this book that you probably wouldn't have gotten if you hadn't been disrupted and invited to reflect? What does this tell you about the value of having a process for disrupting yourself in other activities?

- What rituals do you want to include in your future reading?

Chapter Six

CULTURE

Like capability, culture exerts a strong but indirect influence over how we experience the world and the kinds of effects that we are able to have. Cultures shape our identities, and, often unbeknownst to us, we tend to reciprocate by identifying with our cultures. If we remain unaware of this identification, it can easily trap us in a set of unexamined beliefs.

Culture defines for our particular group what's real, true, acceptable, and desirable, and this affects the kinds of interactions that we can imagine among people and with the world. The pervasive and encompassing nature of culture means that we are, as a rule, blind to its influence on our lives, thoughts, and relationships. Yet, if we want to learn how to change what happens in the world, we need to learn how to observe and shift the working of cultures. Just as culture works indirectly on us, we must work indirectly to change it.

Earlier I said that this book was addressed to well-intentioned people who seek to make the world a better place through the instruments that are available to them, such as business, social activism, or creation of policies and institutions. I also said that most of these efforts are likely to be compromised or fail because they still operate from an old paradigm, within which the world is assembled from discrete pieces, each playing its part in a cosmic machine. Our machine-based metaphors are so pervasive that we hardly notice them: input, output, feedback, leverage, rewiring, reprogramming, metrics, ideal state, and on and on.

A living or regenerative paradigm has a very different character and uses correspondingly different metaphors. It starts with an image of the living, dynamic, and unfolding universe, in which each entity is endowed with the spark of life and an innate capacity for growth and evolution with regard to how it expresses itself. Working from this paradigm, one doesn't attempt to push the world and its inhabitants to an ideal state—that would be coercive and life denying. Rather, one encourages and enables living beings to discover and express their innate potential as contributors to living communities. For those of us who truly want to transform the world, it is the regenerative paradigm that will enable us to do so.

This confronts us with an important question. Are the underlying beliefs, assumptions, patterns, and language that characterize my culture derived from a machine or a living systems paradigm? And if I want to cultivate a living systems culture, what must I do to help with the shift?

LANGUAGE

Language is a key aspect of culture. A culture's terminologies and jargons, its literature and art, and its popular expressions, slang, and memes reveal its values as well as its blind spots. For example, a group that expresses a desire to "evolve incentives for more just and equitable businesses" uses language that demonstrates the value it holds for increasing people's agency and self-determination (a living systems idea). At the same time, its language also reveals a blindness to the fact that incentivization is inherently a command-and-control (or mechanistic) method for effecting change, and thus bound to fail. These internal contradictions shed light on underlying mindsets, concepts, and ways of doing things that must be disrupted in order for something new to manifest.

Close attention to the structure and content of the language that a given culture uses is a doorway to understanding it, and also a doorway for enabling it to transform itself. Most people know this intuitively. Think, for example, of the common reminders to "Use *I* statements," and "Instead of saying *but*, say *and*." The problem with these fairly superficial attempts to modify behavior through modifying language (a mechanistic idea) is that they don't get to the core structure and dynamics of a culture (which requires understanding it as a living system).

As pioneering organizational consultant Peter Drucker famously said, "Culture eats strategy for lunch." In other words, it doesn't matter how good your strategy is if it's not aligned with your culture. Culture is deeper and more powerful and, when misaligned, will block or divert all efforts to move anything forward. This means that whether or not a system can be transformed depends in significant ways on how skillful one is at fostering cultural change. Yet most social or organizational change efforts either fail to take this into account and to provide a basis for recognizing and assessing the culture that is present or have an inadequate grasp of how to evolve it. Culture is both powerful and invisible, and, like every other living entity, it needs to be worked on indirectly.

Following Drucker's admonition, many businesses have tried to take on the question of culture change. But what they've inadvertently done is reinforce the existing culture by working directly on *behavior* change, which is not at all the same as working indirectly on culture change. Managing behavior in order to produce a desired result is a classically mechanistic approach that has the effect of further entrenching top-down systems of command and control while undermining self-accountability and creativity.

By contrast, Phil Jackson very successfully created a team culture based on understanding and developing human potential as a living, dynamic phenomenon. He supplanted an existing, top-down, hierarchical culture ("the coach and the owners know best") with a culture of camaraderie, selflessness, and mutual commitment to a common approach. This called forth the inherent creative and evolutionary capacity of his players. Rather than driving them to produce a *result* (winning), he helped them become dedicated to producing a systemic *effect* (helping young men find a role to play within a common destiny). He was applying what he had learned from Lakota elders, who were very clear about how important it was to help their young people overcome alienation and find a place for themselves in the future of their tribe and nation. For the young men Jackson was working with, society seemed to have no developmental rites of passage that could prepare them for a meaningful place and purpose in the world. Basketball, he saw, could provide such rites of passage.

THE CULTURE TETRAD

One very effective way to work on culture change is by means of a framework that I call the Culture Tetrad.

THE CULTURE TETRAD

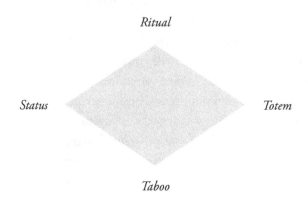

Ritual

Status   *Totem*

Taboo

This framework, which has its source in the study of cultural anthropology, allows one to identify four existing sources from which a culture is drawn and sustained. These sources are what enable a community and its members to maintain alignment and a sense of shared understanding of and language about the world and one another. However, in modern cultures and institutions, these sources are generally invisible and unconscious. If we seek to transform our lives and the ways we work, we first need to bring them into consciousness, understanding their effects and the invisible weave of culture that they produce. This creates the basis from which to evolve more life-enabling sources.

Status determines the distribution of power, based on shared (albeit mostly unconscious) beliefs about where power will do the most good. For example, American culture has long awarded status to people who are White, male, and educated, as well as to people with certain skills (doctors, for example) or roles (such as presidents and CEOs). It also awards status to people who are exceptionally talented, beautiful, or creative. These forms of status tend to attract both wealth and power, which are themselves sources of status, so the process can become self-reinforcing.

Hidden behind the status that specific cultures assign to certain attributes or characteristics is a set of assumptions about what is socially or organizationally beneficial. What attributes are most likely to contribute to the advancement and evolution of a group or a society? What attributes should therefore be encouraged and rewarded?

Assigning status is a culturally useful activity, but it needs to be done carefully to avoid undermining the social values it is intended to reinforce. What would happen if we started to assign status based not so much on what people can do, but instead on the worthwhile challenges they are willing to undertake? That is, what if status came from the significance of the global imperatives that people are willing to connect themselves with, the contributions they are willing to make, and the effectiveness with which they make them?

Here's an example. In my work with Seventh Generation, a company that specializes in ecologically and socially benign household products, we articulated several global imperatives that the company was deeply committed to. One had to do with the recognition that a healthy democracy depends on the critical thinking skills and self-management of its citizenry. Another had to do with understanding that one could only use the natural resources that went into products at the rate that nature could replenish them. The company gave status, in the form of compensation, increased responsibility, and public recognition, to everyone who helped it move these imperatives forward.

Totem is the material representation of the history, essence, cosmology, and future potentiality of a people; a totem's purpose is to evoke the timeless qualities that unify them. For many Indigenous cultures, totems take the form of ancestors who embrace and hold the identity, past and future, of the community. The people of the United States have adopted a variety of totems—George Washington and Abraham Lincoln, the Statue of Liberty, the Bill of Rights, the rugged pioneer, the bootstrap, the ladder to success, and the playing field. Even organizations will at times aspire to have totems. A recognizable example is the Red Cross, a red Greek cross on a white background, which is the symbol for an international organization and is also used to designate emergency medical services and a safe or neutral space in crisis zones.

Given the energetic significance of a totem, there is a great deal of hazard if one aims too low. One of my favorite examples of this is the use of the adjective "purpose-driven" (or its close cousin, "mission-driven") to serve as a self-image for a company. This is another of those instances where language can trip us up. On the surface, being "a purpose-driven business" sounds like a good idea. But, under closer examination, the term directs our attention to an activity in the world rather than the actual nature of the company, and this activity is usually undertaken to address a lack or a failure in some system. This is an impoverished and impoverishing way to represent the *history, essence, cosmology, and future potentiality* of a human enterprise.

By contrast, when I worked with Seventh Generation, it quickly became apparent that *complete transparency* was core to the company's essence and history and to the role it saw itself playing in the world. When in doubt, employees would remind themselves to engage in "complete transparency about everything." This is because they saw themselves as advocates and spokespeople for customers who wanted to take responsibility for the impacts of their household choices. Seventh Generation went out of its way to inform consumers about ingredients and how products were made. When something went wrong with a product, the company publicized the problem and what was being done to correct it rather than trying to hide it. This not only helped to establish strong customer trust and loyalty, but also provided clear guidance with regard to the kind of honesty that was expected of everyone who worked in the company.

Ritual offers a way for cultures to keep their symbols and values alive and meaningful by repeatedly referencing them back to their source in something sacred. By sacred, I mean something that is larger and more significant than us, something that we are willing to set aside our egos and agendas in order to serve. And because I'm using the term in a living systems context, what is sacred is intimately connected to the sourcing of life.

Rituals are the recurring, intentional events that reconnect us to the sacred. An emphasis on intentional connection to what is sacred distinguishes rituals from routines (which are also recurring events). Most cultures create rituals around important life passages, such as birth, death, coming of age, major accomplishment, retirement, and so on. Religious cultures ritualize the celebration of their sacraments. But even a secular organizational culture will recognize that certain values (such as integrity, unity, service, and commitment) arise from a sacred place, and will create rituals that celebrate and rededicate the organization to the intentional pursuit of these values.

While I was working with Seventh Generation, we deliberately replaced one set of company rituals with another. Prior to this, the company had followed the common practice of hosting annual events to recognize and reward certain exemplary employees. The idea was to highlight desirable behaviors and qualities by identifying role models who exhibited them. But, subtly and unintentionally, this undermined the culture they were trying to cultivate by promoting conformity and outward signs of success rather than self-accountability for inner development.

The ritual that replaced this one brought new meaning to the idea of complete transparency by helping people become transparent to themselves. On a monthly basis, everyone would select someone (representing a customer or some other stakeholder) for whom they genuinely wanted to create new benefit. They would write a letter to this person (never mailed) stating the evolution they aspired to create and the new capability they would therefore need to develop. These letters were shared within working teams, fostering communities of mutual support and accountability for the promises the letters articulated. During biannual retreats for the whole company, time was set aside for people to self-report on the growth they experienced as they worked on their promises.

Because Seventh Generation committed fully to this ritual, it eventually had a transformative effect on the organizational culture. Employees stopped looking outside of themselves for validation and recognition from the management team. Instead, they looked inward to identify the meaningful contributions they wanted to pursue and to find the inner resources and agency to pursue them. This growth was collectively celebrated in the form of mutual acknowledgment of the ongoing developmental effort that each person was making within the Seventh Generation community.

Taboo establishes the boundaries for belonging. To violate a taboo is to step outside of what is accepted by a particular culture and to risk censure, punishment, or even banishment. In this way, a taboo sets a limit beyond which no member of the culture is allowed to go.

The challenge with taboos is that they so easily become unconscious and un-examined and can work at cross-purposes to status, totem, and ritual. In my ear-lier Seventh Generation example, the idea of lifting up exemplary employees for recognition subtly conveys the message that it is taboo to make mistakes or do things wrong. But a company dedicated to complete transparency really needed to adopt a taboo against hiding and being ashamed of failures and mistakes. To make this shift required growing a developmental culture within which everyone understood that they were on a learning journey together, inspired by the need to innovate in service to their customers and the planet. This meant that mistakes were inevitable and honorable, so long as they were acknowledged and used as a basis for further learning.

By examining its taboos, making them conscious, and asking what purposes they needed to serve, Seventh Generation was able to evolve its culture to be far more consistent with the beneficial influence it hoped to create in the world. This unleashed an enormous amount of creative energy across the organization, as employees found themselves part of a culture that was unified and coherent and that encouraged them to stretch and grow in service to a shared purpose.

APPLYING THE TETRAD: TWO EXAMPLES

TRADITIONAL BASKETBALL CULTURE

Fame (Ritual)

Ranking (Status)   *Winning (Totem)*

Bad Publicity (Taboo)

In the sport of basketball as a whole, status is assigned to players and teams who achieve the highest rankings and those toward whom scholarships, sponsorships, high salaries, ticket sales, and media attention flow. One totem is the NBA championship ring, which represents a culture unified by the belief that winning is everything. Professional basketball has made fame a sacrament, and it revels in rituals of public recognition—everything from TV appearances to parades to ceremonies recognizing most-valued players to induction into the Naismith Memorial Basketball Hall of Fame. As for taboos, the community comes down hard on anyone who publicly harms or embarrasses the sport through bad publicity arising from doping or sex scandals and other egregious public behaviors. Because the focus is on publicity, there is a secondary taboo around not letting skeletons out of the closet.

PHIL JACKSON'S CHICAGO BULLS CULTURE

Spiritualizing the Game (Ritual)

*Rising Together
(Status)*

*Presence to the Moment
(Totem)*

Self-Aggrandizement (Taboo)

It is illuminating to contrast the culture tetrad for basketball to the tetrad that describes the culture Phil Jackson was creating with his teams.

Against this larger cultural background, Phil Jackson's attempts to cultivate a completely alternative culture must at first have seemed quixotic. His teams gave status to players who helped their teammates raise their averages, so that everyone could rise together. The Bulls' totem was mindfulness, presence to what was unfolding in the moment, rather than conformance to preestablished patterns of play. On behalf of the young people coming up behind them, the team put a great deal of effort into spiritualizing the game itself, engaging in collective rituals around breathing, meditation, reflection, and self-accountability. And they made self-aggrandizement taboo, discouraging the archetype of the single heroic player in favor of the power and intelligence that could only come through unified effort.

SIXTH INTERMEZZO

Use the Culture Tetrad to reflect on the family, organizational, or other cultures that unconsciously influence your thinking. How have these influences affected your reading process?

- Those things that attract our attention, energy, and effort are indicators of what we give status to. When you look back over your journal, what do your notes reveal about where your attention is and thus what carries status in your life? Can you see a pattern of influence with regard to your mindset that inspired you to underline some things and be annoyed by others?

- What metaphors do you most often use to describe your life—your job, pastimes, family, self? Where did these metaphors come from, and what do they point to with regard to the symbols or totems you use? Are they the right symbols? That is, do they really represent the level at which you aspire to live your life? And how are these metaphors, totems, and symbols shaping your reading of this book?

- Review your work on previous intermezzos. What rituals did you engage in as you read and journaled? How did they create the mindset that framed your thinking about what you read and what you recorded?

- What is taboo in your life, including your family or workplace? How have these taboos affected the judgments you've made about this book's content? How do they influence your mindset and thinking as you read and journal?

CHAPTER SEVEN

CONSCIOUSNESS

Along with *capability* and *culture*, the third key dimension of indirect work is the development of a method for evoking *consciousness*, which works on the actor rather than the action. I believe that the capacity for consciousness is one of the primary things that differentiates the human species. One might characterize it as the thread that we contribute to the weave of evolution. When we fail to develop our own and others' potential for consciousness, then we also fail to play our role within the unfolding processes of life on our planet.

Consciousness is the necessary antidote to our overwhelming tendency to engage in automatic habits of thought and behavior. In its absence, these habits extend to the most general reaches of our collective understanding of the universe itself, conceived of by Western Europeans in the time of the Renaissance as a giant clockwork. This peculiarity of regional imagination has now become the dominant paradigm of reality worldwide. As such, it has created a self-reinforcing loop in which the mechanistic universe is reflected in the conceptualization of our bodies and minds as biological machines and our institutions as social machines. Thus, we invent mechanistic metaphors and processes for educating and healing ourselves. In other words, we resort to conditioning, a default approach that is precisely the opposite of living free, self-determined human lives. And, in a mechanical feedback process, this conditioning reinforces the already prevalent tendency toward automatism.

As I noted above, cultures reinforce the paradigms that they derive from. Cultures are pervasive, and their operations are, for the most part, indirect and invisible to us, and so we can easily fall back into an undesirable paradigm without realizing it. We need to learn how to disrupt these automatic patterns, often reminding ourselves and one another to "Snap out of it! Wake up!"

Establishing a strong, ongoing intention to become conscious is the necessary first step toward habituating ourselves to continually observe our thinking patterns, trace them back to old sources, and replace these sources with new ones for higher-level thinking and imaging. It takes an equally strong and ongoing intention to cultivate a culture that values and fosters this mental discipline. The awakening of consciousness is not a one-time thing; it needs to be renewed again and again, just as we have to restart our cars every time we want to drive them.

From a regenerative perspective, consciousness is a prerequisite for individuals' and groups' evolutionary growth, which depends on the capability to recognize and access different orders or levels of mind (described in chapter 5 as exponential powers of understanding). Consciousness also enables the concentration needed to penetrate the illusion of a world of disparate, fragmented objects—cogs and wheels—in order to grasp the underlying dynamism and relatedness that knits the world into a living whole.

Consciousness How-To

The necessity for developing consciousness is not a particularly original thought. Across the ages, teachers and sages taught a host of esoteric disciplines and practices toward this end. Nevertheless, when I describe the centrality of consciousness to the work of making change in the world, the first response I hear is usually, "Yeah, great, but how do we do it?" This is why I emphasize the need for a practical method that can be applied within the contexts of personal life and work, as an *indirect* approach to broader change.

The method includes three practices for awakening and developing consciousness. First, we wake ourselves up whenever our tendency to go on automatic threatens to undermine the activity we're engaged in. Second, we need to remain connected to the overwhelming, interwoven, awe-inspiring wholeness and nestedness of reality rather than breaking the universe into abstract fragments for our convenience. Third, we need to climb up the levels of mind—from thing mind to process mind to essence mind to sourcing mind.

First Principles

One way to work on these three practices is by use of a framework that I call the Seven First Principles of Regeneration. Application of this framework could be thought of as an exercise for awakening and maintaining consciousness with regard to the world as a living, whole phenomenon. We can bring it to any activity or relationship as a way to observe and step outside of our thinking in order to assess and upgrade its quality. In what follows, I will introduce each of the seven principles alongside its opposite, which can be thought of as its parallel within a mechanistic worldview. The contrast is intended to bring the principles to life, enabling us to recognize when we've dropped into a lower level of mind and hoist ourselves back up to a higher level. This is the essential work of consciousness. Please keep in mind that, although the framework is represented here as a diagram, it describes what is actually an interwoven, living whole. It is also very easy to take it in as a list or a collection, which treats the different concepts as separate fragments. But the principles only really work to build consciousness when we remain aware of their nature and apply them together as an indivisible whole thought.

Seven First Principles of Regeneration

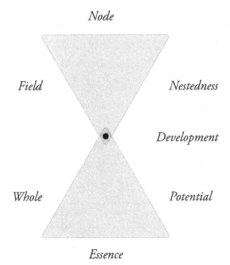

Node

Field   *Nestedness*

Development

Whole   *Potential*

Essence

Whole (versus fragment). Thinking about our world, our work, and ourselves in terms of fragments has become so ubiquitous that we are hardly aware of it. Many of us have been told since childhood, "If you want to solve a problem, break it down into its component parts." We do this with regard to almost everything. Days are broken into hours and minutes. Schools teach to the test. Companies set targets to measure. Parents seek to manage the behaviors of their children, while employers manage the behaviors of employees. Governments make lists of problems to solve and then prioritize them. The pattern is everywhere we look. Fragmentation is seductive because it promotes the illusion that simplicity and progress can be achieved by direct action, where specific problems get resolved and specific results delivered. But direct action is always partial, and it always creates unintended consequences.

Moreover, though it might affect a system's functions, it can't transform its state. To do this requires understanding and engaging with the system as a *whole*, which I believe is the foundation for remaining grounded in reality. As far as life is concerned, wholes are real; fragments are abstract fictions. You can't dissect and reassemble a frog and still have a frog. But we've been so thoroughly conditioned to dissect, dismantle, and list reality that it can be almost impossibly difficult to recognize when we've done so.

In spite of this, each of us has the innate capacity to experience wholes. When I connect with someone I deeply love, I experience and have affection for them as a whole being. It doesn't even occur to me to question their right to be whole and alive. My heart simply accepts their unity, and this creates a distinctive state within my mind—a being-to-being encounter—which means that I am showing up as a whole being as well.

Here's a practical example of what I mean. My 10-year-old, joyously open-adopted granddaughter is one of the people I deeply love. This means that I am strongly motivated to engage with her as a whole human being. When she wants to do something like set the table, I have to overcome my anxiety that she's going to drop one of the plates and instead try to understand the source of her desire. Clearly, she wants to show that she's part of her whole, melded family, and making the table beautiful is her way of playing a contributing role. At the same time, she has to play this role in a way that actually enables us to accomplish what we're trying to do, which is to have meals that bring us together comfortably and harmoniously. Accommodating our range of differences is a challenge for a young child with a strong aesthetic compass, and it is in the ways that she rises to these challenges that I get an undeniable sense of her as her own being.

She has chosen the role of table setter as an expression of her capacity to be self-determining. This is very different from me giving her a task to do in order to encourage and train her to be responsible. Her aspiration in all of this is clearly evident—to create beauty and bring joy to others. Yes, she's likely to fall short as she learns and develops into what she's trying to be. Dishes may get dropped from time to time. But this is how the whole of her finds a way to become and express itself. So long as I can stay true to the aspirations in her and in me, I can be with her in the process.

It's easy to see a "wholistic" process like this at work with someone who is close. But how do we bring the same kind of consciousness to subjects, people, and other entities with whom we don't have a natural affinity or may even be in conflict? Basically, the same way. We seek to understand what they are trying to achieve in terms of their need to be self-determining, their aspirations, and the role they are trying to play within a larger system that is pursuing a purpose. If we can learn to do this consistently, we have an almost foolproof way of engaging with everyone and everything as a living whole.

Essence (versus category). Fragmentation is the original sin of mechanistic thinking and the source of its degenerative effects. Once we've broken wholes into fragments, we've dropped out of a living, whole-fabric understanding of the world, and suddenly we're faced with a host of constantly proliferating pieces and parts. Faced with this, the mind understandably boggles. It seeks a way to organize the chaos of fragmentary experience by sorting it into categories, putting like with like, and discarding whatever upsets our sense of order. This profoundly shapes our experience of reality. We replace real phenomena with abstract ideas, for example substituting demographic categories for the actual person standing in front of us. They go from being *themself* to being a cisgender female, Caucasian, middle-child, middle-income, college-educated, average height, jogger, parent of two, social worker, with a family history of diabetes, *etcetera, etcetera, etcetera, ad infinitum.*

This process is so deeply conditioned in us and so deeply embedded in our language that we can hardly see it happening, let alone recognize its consequences. It is a form of mental murder, intellectually dissecting and dismembering living beings until there's no being left. Then, from the artificial constructs with which we have replaced living beings, we build systems of analysis, research, policy making, education, marketing, land management, health care, and incarceration. And, when these systems create new problems, we use the same artificial methods to repair them.

"Now wait a minute!" I regularly hear people object. "There's no way to manage the complexities of society or nature or governance if we can't generalize." This is true if one is operating in a world of fragments, which inevitably complicates what one is trying to do. Generalizing phenomena into categories is a way of simplifying a complicated situation. But in a living systems world, every entity is managing itself, based on its *essence*, in response to and in creative collaboration with its complex surroundings. Living beings and processes have evolved to generate and work with complexity. For the human mind, managing complexity (as opposed to complicatedness) requires discerning the source of what makes things whole and intelligible. I call this discernment process *revealing the essence* of something.

To reveal essence, I seek to understand the working of a whole, by which I mean how it goes about playing a contributing role within the value-adding process of a larger whole. When I look across time, I find that I can recognize certain characteristic patterns in the roles that a living system will choose and the ways it goes about playing them. This gives me insight into its essence.

From the time when my granddaughter was a toddler, I could see her attraction to color, beauty, and arranging things into harmonious patterns. On the surface, this could be interpreted as a personality trait or a talent. But it goes deeper than this. When she volunteers to set our family dinner table, she's attempting to bring integration between the inner meaning of the activity (harmonization) and its outward expression (a cluttered table surrounded by diverse people).

When she was younger, her efforts seemed tyrannical: "No one is allowed to leave bowls on the table!" But as she's learned to temper her own willfulness and take into account the different needs and purposes of her family members, she has learned to create table settings that really do harmonize all of those purposes. This has channeled her creativity toward more sophisticated design challenges, while at the same time making more evident her aspirational impulse to integrate inner and outer meanings.

Like any child, my granddaughter is a complex being, expressing herself through a baffling array of seemingly unrelated behaviors. But once I understood the essence that is seeking to be expressed through these behaviors, and the search to find appropriate ways to connect this essence to family and school, her life and wholeness became self-evident to me. And I can now find powerful new ways to play my role as grandmother in support of her essence.

Potential (versus problem). One of the less obvious consequences of fragmentation is the way it causes us to view the world in terms of problems. Because fragmentation drives us to categorize things, and because living phenomena can never be reduced to the generic categories by which we try to manage them, problems become inevitable. You might say that the definition of a problem is the difference between what we think something should be, as defined by the categories we put it in, and what it actually is.

This affects how we think about change. In a fragmented, categorized, and genericized world, one undertakes change in order to fix problems and bring everything into a more ideal state. We attempt to remake the real world in the image of our abstractions. It's small wonder that this process almost always yields unintended consequences in the form of new problems to solve.

On reflection, I'm guessing that most of us can see how prevalent this problem-solving orientation is and how it even determines our definitions of ideas like pragmatism and success. But what happens if we shift our orientation from problem to *potential?* In living systems, potential arises from the relationship between a specific whole (and the essence that organizes its working) and the value-adding process of a larger whole. In other words, one realizes potential when one can see how the essence of something can lead it to make a contribution to a larger system's ability to evolve its essence expression in a value-generating way.

This is the dynamic unfolding in my story about my granddaughter and the dinner table—the realization of new potential by helping her find ways to put her essence to work in service to a larger family purpose. This wasn't a given; it was something we had to discover and work on together. After all, many parents would experience the behaviors of a strong-willed, opinionated little girl as a problem. Some might discipline a child to try to break perceived patterns of rudeness or dominance. Others might negotiate a truce: "You can set the table any way you like, once every week." But neither approach does anything to connect with her potential and develop its expression.

In my granddaughter's case, the key was getting her to think about the other people who were going to participate in the meal. What would make her older brother feel included in a harmonious experience? Her parents? Dinner guests? What would facilitate the work of whoever was preparing the meal? Instead of banishing the unsightly collection of condiments from the table, could she find creative ways to present them? Instead of icing the cake herself, could she find a way to orchestrate a collective decorating activity, so that everyone could contribute?

Questions like these, which are designed to foster her self-determination and self-management, have also created the conditions under which her essence can be welcomed fully into the collective process of family meals. She's found a way to connect her own aspirations for beauty to making life better for everyone. And the process is just beginning; together we've discovered a path by which her creativity can continue to evolve to address increasingly interesting, complex, and meaningful challenges.

Development (versus determinism). One consequence of the clockwork view of reality is determinism. That is, if we can describe all of the variables in a situation, then we will be able to accurately predict in advance what will occur. We know from experience that this can't ever be entirely true, either because it is simply impossible to know all of the variables or because of the influences of chaos and entropy. Nevertheless, we assume the general legitimacy of our machine metaphor and make accommodations for a bit of unpredictability in the system.

This determinism is applied wholesale to our understanding of human beings, perceived as the products of genetic inheritance, social conditioning, and/or a destiny ordained by God (or gods, as the case may be). Whether we attribute the source of a person's character to nature or nurture or both, we assume that it is mostly fixed. People reflect the traits and talents they were born with or raised to, and we must either accept, celebrate, or punish them for this.

Racism, sexism, and heterosexism, which hold that certain people will exhibit specific characteristics, limits, or inferiority as a direct result of their birth, are obvious, exaggerated examples of this kind of determinism. But, in fact, bias is ubiquitous in how we organize every aspect of our society, from IQ tests to social welfare policies and from employee evaluations to chains of command. Once we accept the idea that demographic categories and aptitude tests are reasonable ways to describe people, it's a short step to viewing them as cogs and levers in a machine and managing them accordingly. Within a deterministic culture, it not only becomes impossible to think of and treat people as whole beings with their own essences and potentials; it also becomes impossible to think of any entity or system in this way. In other words, living systems consciousness cannot be imported as an intellectual idea. It has to be internalized as a way of being.

This is the role of *development*, to cultivate the capacities for self-observation and conscious choice that enable us to show up as living, creative beings in a living, creative world, to be self-determining rather than predetermined. Development, in other words, is not the same thing as training or knowledge transfer, which are direct ways of working. Development works on our ability to be awake with regard to ourselves, and this is inherently indirect. We become aware of and selective about the influences that shape our thinking and experiencing. We learn to anticipate the systemic effects we produce through our choices and actions. We grow the creative capacity to make new, unanticipated choices based on our evolving understanding of an evolving world.

As grandmother, one of the key roles I play in my granddaughter's life is to help her develop her own capacity to be consciously self-determining. We share a private joke about the fact that I like to ask her "unanswerable questions." At age 10, her artistic spirit takes the form of a tornado most of the time, energetic as hell but not especially focused or self-aware. When I ask her why she's chosen the elements and colors she wants to bring together in a painting or outfit or table setting, it's not because there is any right answer to my question. I am not interested in intervening in a direct way or getting her to see something in particular. Rather, I want to help her become more reflective, to learn to swim upstream in her own creative process. When, as happens on occasion, she responds, "Because I want to!" I accept this as a perfectly valid answer because it is as good a starting point as any for her to play with what she wants and why. I'm simply inviting her into the awareness that she can make choices and set her own direction in life.

At the same time, I often invite her to reflect on the effects she wants to create. What kind of dinner experience will her dad have, given how she's arranging tonight's table? How is that going to be different from last night's? Is the effect she wants to create reflected in the choices she's made? Again, these are open-ended questions, with no correct answers. They are intended to help her experience her connections with others and the way her own agency can bring more life into these connections.

There's an important and easily missed nuance to what I'm doing with my granddaughter. She and I don't have these conversations in the hurly-burly of daily life. Instead, we set aside time to focus on something that she's chosen to work on in a way that allows me to indirectly work on her ability to manage herself in life. It's our own little ceremony of reflection, and it happens almost every week. This is very different from seizing teaching moments, in which an adult intervenes with a child in the middle of an activity in order to reinforce a positive pattern or break a negative one. A classically behaviorist idea, teaching moments are designed to condition certain patterns of behavior and are therefore anti-developmental. I'm trying to do the opposite—to help my granddaughter consciously reflect so that she becomes increasingly able to manage her behaviors based on her own discernment and choices.

On more than one occasion I've had someone misinterpret what I mean by this. "Oh," they say, "you mean that you go back and work with your granddaughter on the behavior issue later, when things are quieter."

"No, that's not it at all!" I respond. I never refer to a specific event, even if I have an opinion about it. It's simply none of my business. That would be a direct way of working, and I would be trying to correct her. That's manipulation, not development. I have to rein in any temptation I might have to supply her with my thoughts and instead help her work on her ability to generate better-quality thoughts for herself.

This is exactly what I do when I'm working with anyone, from student to CEO. I never intervene in the content of what they are working on. I certainly don't try to teach them to be more sustainability-minded or socially responsible. I only offer myself as a resource for the development of the consciousness they need to be truly effective. They can take it from there, and they do!

At this point in a progression through the seven first principles framework, I always experience a shift in focus. As I mentioned earlier, I use this framework as a way to invoke and develop consciousness. Regardless of what I'm working on, it helps me to be more conscious in my approach. I find that the first three terms—whole, potential, essence—help me understand and engage with what I'm working on as a living entity, in and of itself. With the final three terms, I shift my attention to the aspect of its livingness that is all about being embedded within a larger context, a shift that greatly complexifies and enriches my understanding. The middle term, development, bridges these two aspects because it works on growing the capacity of a living entity first to be itself and second to make a contribution to its world.

To illustrate the first four terms, I drew on an aspect of my relationship with my granddaughter because these ideas are often more easily understood when applied to children. However, because of her young age, my granddaughter is not yet consciously engaged with or able to form clear intentions about her world and future path within it. For this reason, I now want to introduce an example from my work in the corporate world.

Over quite a few years, I have worked with Jeffrey Hollender, founder of Seventh Generation, a company specializing in nontoxic, ecologically benign household and personal products. From his core, Hollender is committed to radical transparency, social justice, and exposing dissonance between what people say and what they do. This made for a compelling and visionary company that attracted good people. But when I first met Hollender, Seventh Generation was very much operating at the level of well-meaning organization—lots of aspirations and activity but not enough effectiveness with regard to creating real transformational change.

Together we worked on developing Hollender's ability and the ability of his organization to see customers, suppliers, distributors, and markets as living beings longing to realize more of their own essences and potentials. This shift in perspective and paradigm unleashed the caring and creativity of Seventh Generation's people. The corresponding evolution in the efficacy of its products made it an influential change leader in its field.

Even as this transformation was occurring in Seventh Generation, Hollender was increasingly seeing how change might happen at a larger, society-wide scale. He intuited that that business had a critical role to play in a democratic society but was lacking the necessary frameworks and institutions for working on it. He was beginning, in other words, to define a new whole for himself to work on: business itself. Having tried to work on social and governmental change from within a single company and its relationship to customers, Hollender recognized that far more potential could be realized by stepping out of Seventh Generation to work at the next level up, in the larger field of business as a whole. At this point, I will pick up the thread of his story and look at it through the lens of the remaining three terms in our framework.

———————

Nestedness (versus progressive aggregation). Anyone who sincerely wants to contribute to making the world a better place but is trying to do so from a non-living-systems worldview faces a growing number of methods and best practices in the field. After all, as I write this book, people everywhere are applying a huge amount of human intelligence and effort to solving the world's many urgent problems. Without the internal mental shift that engages wholes rather than fragments, and essence rather than categories, well-meaning people everywhere find themselves collecting and aggregating the tools that they believe are most likely to create progress. However, these tools themselves are often fragmented and thus are actually contributing to fragmentation—for example, efforts to address racial justice that are undertaken independently of or even in opposition to environmental considerations. Yet most people accept them into their toolkits because something, after all, is better than nothing. What they don't realize is that this only serves to reinforce the paradigmatic failures that are the source of the problems in the first place.

Many people are aware of this issue, of course, and have attempted to address it through systems thinking, by identifying, mapping, and designing for the connections among elements within a system and at different levels of system. An example of this is current, extensive work on connecting the dots between agricultural practice, habitat restoration, seed sovereignty, carbon sequestration, farmworker rights, regional economies, equitable access to nourishing food, and multiple other concerns of regenerative ag.

Such efforts to integrate multiple, diverse needs and bodies of knowledge are a hallmark of good design and can certainly lead to more sophisticated, holistic solutions and policies. But the process of accretion of information and action, no matter how comprehensive, will never on its own generate the shift in perspective that allows us to engage with a living whole. If anything, the tendency to aggregate and integrate only serves to reinforce the problems associated with fragmentation. This is because it derives its raw materials from the underlying practice of breaking things down into parts in order to understand them before attempting to reassemble them into something that makes sense.

By contrast, when we leave behind the world of fragments and anchor our thinking in the experience of something whole, then we can see it in relation to its essence, potential, and development. This gives us a completely different basis from which to work with its complexities, which can be understood not only in terms of its own wholeness but also with regard to its nestedness within other wholes. From the perspective of *nestedness*, a living whole will always be nested within larger living wholes, which provide the conditions necessary for life. By definition, the larger whole is not a collection of elements (or fragments), any more than the smaller whole is. This means that the beingness of the smaller whole is, in reality, an aspect of the beingness of the larger whole.

Of course, this insight extends up and down multiples levels of nested wholes, so that being and identity are to some extent shared among them. One of the reasons that, when I'm being conscious, I can care unconditionally for my family is that in some sense I *am one with* and indivisible from my family (or my community or my nation). The divisions we make between ourselves and the systems we are nested in are at times useful, but they are also arbitrary. We are inextricably intertwined with Nature and she with us; to imagine, for example, that we could continue to breathe if Earth's forests and oceans weren't breathing back to us is a dangerous fallacy. This absolute interdependence of life, this inter-beingness, is what Indigenous peoples have been trying to convey to the rest of us for centuries.

When we experience an entity as a nested living system, we are able to understand it at work, as it seeks to contribute to a larger system. We also see the larger system working to contribute to an even larger system. For example, when I invest my energy and work to help a company realize more of its potential, I'm helping it to evolve the contributions it will make to the lives of its customers, workers, industry, or (depending on its ambition) nation. To the degree that I can be intelligent with my investment, maintaining consciousness of the life of the entity I'm working in and the role it is seeking to play in the lives of larger systems, then my relatively modest actions can translate into large effects. This is different from the machine-based metaphor of targeted intervention, which assumes that the right force applied at the right point in a system can yield disproportionate impact. Rather, I am describing an indirect outcome of understanding and working with wholes, alive and nested, that are expressing their innate drive to contribute.

In founding Seventh Generation, Jeffrey Hollender took a stand against what he saw as the evils of corporations. He wanted to create a company that aligned with his ecological and social values and offered a stark contrast to business as usual. But what he couldn't see was how polarizing this position was and how it cut him off from his true potential as a change agent. Like so many of his peers, he was trying to transform the world by fragmenting it into good guys and bad guys.

I remember that we talked about this one night over dinner. Hollender wanted to know how I had been able to work in large multinational corporations without dropping into judgment and polarization. "Well," I told him, "I didn't think of any of the individuals I was working with as bad people. They simply lacked capability. I looked at each person as someone who wanted to do something worthwhile, and I tried to figure out how to build the capabilities they would need to get where they were trying to go."

Afterward, as he continued to ponder his question, Hollender realized how much more effective he could be if he could engage with the corporate world instead of pushing it away. Rather than focusing on his own company and the small group of allied businesses that were striving for greater corporate responsibility, he began to see himself as connected to and working within a greater whole. By adopting the attitude that nearly every business is trying to make a worthwhile contribution to at least the immediate lives of its customers, he entered into working relationships that influenced some of the most powerful companies in the world. It's interesting to note that this change in scale of nested system was accompanied by a change in perspective. Referring back to exponential powers of understanding and the levels of mind metaphor (chapter 5), Hollender had shifted from thing mind to process mind, with a focus on connectedness and dynamism.

This change, significant though it may have been, was only a stepping-stone in Hollender's development. It wasn't long before he came to realize that working with one company at a time to support change was too slow and failed to produce the kind of systemic evolution that he was aiming for. He began to see the need to bring a broad alliance of companies together to actually shift the direction of governing systems and processes. By working together developmentally, businesses could learn from one another and influence national (and international) policy in a way that no individual company could on its own. This was the origin of the American Sustainable Business Council (ASBC), which Hollender cofounded with social entrepreneur and educational pioneer David Levine.

This shift to a greater *governing* whole was also accompanied by a second mental shift—from process to essence mind. Through deep reflection, Hollender and his colleagues were able to articulate the essence of governing as "creating a society that works for all." The problem now is that the political system has become so profoundly polarized that it's hard for it to do this essential work.

Hollender was convinced that the business community had a critical, essence-sourced role to play in evolving governing processes because what business-es of every stripe have in common is their experience of engaging with wholes. Successful businesses learn to understand and respond to the lives and evolving aspirations of the people and groups they serve. Polarization and fragmentation are the antithesis of good business practice, which seeks to bring people together around a product rather than driving them apart over ideological or cultural dif-ferences. There is, of course, wide variation in the sophistication and holism with which companies come to understand their markets, but there is nearly universal agreement about the need to do so.

ASBC set out to implement this insight by enabling the business sector to bring its unique perspective to bear on the development of governing processes that would actually result in a society that works for all. Any business with a sincere desire to work on this question was invited to participate, regardless of its politi-cal orientation, because diversity of perspective was valued as a powerful creative instrument. Through dialogue, collective learning, and an iterative process for articulating positions and white papers, the ASBC was able over time to create a whole, singular, and therefore influential voice on behalf of its members

Node (versus scale). It appears that these days people are obsessed with the idea of scalability. They seem shocked when I counter that taking practices to scale is a life-denying way of thinking, an insidious and destructive expression of the mech-anistic worldview. For most of the people I engage with, it's impossible to imagine making the kinds of global changes that are needed (or, for that matter, to create a successful business) if we don't collect good solutions and take them to scale.

But this is precisely the problem with the idea of scale. These good solutions might be perfect in a particular situation, but when indiscriminately applied, they become generic. Scalability has to do with imposing an imported idea of what's right and good, a so-called best practice, rather than starting from the essence and wholeness of distinctive living entities. We can easily recognize this problem in specific cases, such as universal education standards that leave individual children behind or international development programs committed to the creation of gen-eral benefits that instead lead to displacement of local people and degradation of local cultures and ecosystems. But even in the face of these and other widespread failures, the idea of scalability is very hard to shake loose from because it is so dif-ficult to envision a different way to work on significant, lasting change.

From a living systems perspective, the answer to this dilemma lies in our ability to recognize *nodes*, those places within a specific system where the introduction of new energy or a different quality of energy will enable an evolution and expression of its potential. I am using the term differently from the conventional mechanistic understanding of nodes as places in a network where multiple intersections occur. For me, nodes are about energization, like acupuncture points rather than superhighway cloverleafs. When I have helped business organizations awaken to their essence and discover the potential for contribution that could flow from living this essence, the effect has been highly energizing, sometimes healing, always transformative, and therefore always nodal.

Like all of the other terms in this framework, nodal thinking requires consciousness. It asks that we understand a given system in terms of its livingness or, as I sometimes say, its *working*. In order to understand a system's working, I have to look beyond the sensory data (which are by definition fragments) in order to form a mental image of what's happening with the system as it engages dynamically with its context. I'm seeking to experience the *energies* that are the source of the whole phenomenon I perceive, and this requires conscious attention.

Nodal thinking addresses problems of scale because it can be applied to systems of any scale. The key is to understand the system as alive, whole, and imbued with potential, and to use this understanding as a basis for discovering the node or nodes that will energize it. This is as true for a child or a kindergarten classroom as it is for the governance of a nation. The inner process requires commitment, openness, and humility, and each of us will find some systems easier to read than others, but the fundamental approach is the same regardless of the size of what we are thinking about.

I mentioned earlier that Jeffrey Hollender, in his role as a founding member of the ASBC, was seeking to shift the scale of his influence by taking on a larger whole, in this case the governing institutions that shape regional, national, and international policy. He and his cofounder had a very powerful business community behind them, but the trick was to find the right nodal intervention. In my conversations with Hollender as he was going through this process, it was exciting to hear how the group's thinking was evolving.

They began with the idea of countering the influence of lobbying by corporate and other interest groups. "We need to become the counter-lobbyists," they insisted. "We need to offer the other half of the story." With this framing, they were still operating within a polarized paradigm of good and bad actors. Nevertheless, by taking on the persona of lobbyists, they had accepted the idea of advocacy as an appropriate way to interface with governing bodies.

The next big step was to radically reframe the idea of advocacy. The reason that they had objected to corporate lobbying was that it was partial. They realized that, by trying to advocate for an opposing position, they were being just as partial. They began to envision a role for themselves as advocates for the whole picture. The ASBC would work on educating legislators and other stakeholders to understand all of the systemic implications of an issue or piece of legislation. This would give them what they needed to make good decisions on behalf of society as a whole, but the rest was up to them.

The ASBC's approach was rigorously systemic, focusing on the whole of what it takes to govern in a way that creates a nation that serves all. Active dialogue, which encourages participants to form a more comprehensive understanding of a whole, was given preference over debate, tolerance, or inclusion, all of which encourage people to defend their narrow positions. This was ASBC's nodal intervention, which it came to call *educational advocacy*. It was a good illustration of what I mean by indirect work because it set aside pressuring people to adopt a particular position in favor of growing their ability to think about things in a truly whole way.

Field (versus transaction). One of the most debilitating outcomes of approaching life from a mechanistic perspective is that we end up in a *transactional* world, one in which we perpetually have to negotiate for what we need. This is the inevitable result of a cascade of life-denying processes—from fragmentation to categorization and from determinism to scaling. In a transactional world, exchanges are measured according to *what's in it for me?* We cultivate vigilance around getting as much as possible while giving away as little as necessary. Put another way, we become deeply, and often unconsciously, conditioned to extract value—from the products and services we buy, the planet we live on, the institutions that serve us, and the people around us.

At first, this might seem like an exaggeration, but it's a ubiquitous phenomenon, even in intimate relationships. Employers or clients lean on employees to get the most out of them, and employees lean in turn on those who are lower down the chain. Parents push their kids to do well on tests so that they can gain access to educational opportunities that will secure their position in some future economy. Lovers and friends ask each other, "What have you done for me lately?" Then there is the way we treat Earth, where intersecting ecological catastrophes caused by centuries of value extraction demand a collective, caring response but we can't seem to rise above a transactional mindset.

This transactional orthodoxy arises from fear—the fear of not having or being enough and the fear of being taken advantage of. These fears, in turn, lead to struggles over power. In a worldview of scarcity, one that has trouble contemplating the unlimited creative potentialities of evolution, gaining power over other things and people is the only way to ensure that we have enough. This makes sense in a mechanistic universe, where entropy rules and life is a zero-sum game.

Of course, many people recoil at the prospect of a purely transactional life. This book, after all, is directed to well-meaning people, people who care about philanthropy, social change, and an increasingly just and sustainable world. Altruism seems to be innate in human beings, but when we seek to contribute to society, our altruism tends to take fragmented or reactive forms. Sometimes we set out to right wrongs by marching in the streets or pushing for legislative reforms. This focus on problems whose sources are in past actions and decisions is backward looking and reactive; its effects are limited to *arresting disorder*. Alternatively, people may seek to create something better, for example through tree-planting campaigns or improving access to health care or education for disadvantaged communities, a *do-good* orientation. Neither approach, as I pointed out at the beginning of this book, is likely to be effective in the long run, mainly because so many of our actions actually produce the opposite of what we aim for. This is an effect of our lack of education and experience working with living wholes.

Fields, the final term in our seven-term framework, is a way of referring to the totality of energies present in a system that give rise to the phenomena that we observe. This totality includes material energies like gravity, light, sound, molecular bonding, and physical motion. It also includes mental and cultural energies like thought, emotion, historical resonance, and spiritual experience. In quantum theory, fields are the energetic substrate (or implicate order, in David Bohm's conceptualization) from which excited states of energy give rise to what we experience as physical particles—the building blocks of an apparently material universe. This substrate—which is the direction point on the Theory of Change Tetrad—is a deeper level of reality and the basis for the idea of indirect work. If we can learn to influence the underlying energetic pattern, we can profoundly shift the resulting phenomena.

One of the implications of this way of thinking, and one of the reasons that we can put it to practical use, is that we really are one with our universe. We, along with everything that we experience, are all expressions arising out of a unified energetic field, which means that we simultaneously shape and are shaped by it. It also means that we can have an influence on things without directly touching them, a fact reflected in the idea of the ripple effect. Consciousness, if we are willing to develop it, enables us to engage in this field, influencing it in an intentional way in order to create more whole and life-affirming patterns.

I believe that the experience of fields is commonplace, but we lack adequate language for describing or working with them. For example, we've probably all walked into a crowded room and been able to pick up on the underlying dynamics—tense, celebratory, sad, silly, highly focused. Most of us have also probably had the personal experience of shifting a dynamic through our own state of being, for example by providing a stable and caring presence during a conflict or crisis. We may also know the feeling of shifting country or job, encountering a striking new culture. Thinking of a field as a container within which events occur helps us see that its quality or state has an enormous effect on what can be made or helped to arise within it (although the container metaphor is not quite right because fields have unlimited extension). The art of indirect work, then, has everything to do with learning to shift the qualities or states of fields.

Jeffrey Hollender and the ASBC team had settled on educational advocacy as the nodal intervention that would allow them to shift governing processes across a wide array of governmental bodies. But given how polarized and conflicted politics had become, they knew they would need to create the right field, a space outside of the usual debates and posturing where a more unifying vision could emerge. Having established their main offices in Washington, DC, they evolved three different kinds of event, each offered on a recurring cycle. These were carefully designed and facilitated to challenge business as usual in Washington by fostering dialogue, the process by which different perspectives evolve toward a shared and more encompassing understanding. All points of view were welcome, but always solicited within a framework for creating shared intelligence about the whole of an issue.

The group hosted large membership gatherings, designed as conversations rather than as staged events with talking heads presenting contrasting opinions. The idea was to underscore that each member could draw on their own experience and intelligence in order to rise to the challenges presented by the state of the world. Instead of putting experts at the front of a room, they sat people around tables and provided provocative questions to work on. They paid a great deal of attention to framing these questions in ways that would evoke consciousness and conscientiousness rather than polarization, and encourage reflection rather than positioning. In this way, participants became increasingly skillful contributors to meaningful dialogue.

For smaller, more deep-dive conversations, they invited a variety of stakeholders (with special attention paid to policy makers) to think together about a subject of particular interest, such as voting rights. Again, the object was to grow the holistic understanding of policy makers rather than to push them to adopt specific positions. In this way, one could say that ASBC offered a refreshing counterpoint and antidote to the constant drumbeat of lobbying that dominates discourse in the United States capitol. Their conversations managed to regenerate a field within which rigor and thoughtfulness became not only possible but mutually expected, thereby creating the kind of consideration that is appropriate for critically important topics.

Finally, ASBC published a series of position papers that were also generated through conversations among its members. Rather than writing a majority opinion, with dissenting opinions noted or included, the idea was to use the shared aim of building a democracy that works for all to generate a collective understanding. A member of the executive team, often Hollender, would circulate to the membership an initial draft for a paper. A series of online sessions were then held to deepen the thinking, after which the paper would be rewritten and recirculated. Participants were invited to reflect on how their own thinking was evolving in relation to the collective thinking. This awareness helped build faith that evolution was possible—critically important when it came to polarizing issues—and it nurtured a field of hope.

CONSCIOUSNESS ON THE COURT

When I read Phil Jackson's books and watch the interviews that he's given over the years, it seems obvious to me that the development of consciousness is at the core of everything he does. More important, in Jackson's understanding, consciousness is not just something one taps into during quiet meditation in tranquil settings. It can be accessed right in the heat of things, bringing agency and self-management to everything from the fast-paced intensity of a basketball game to raising children to driving in heavy traffic to flourishing creatively in a go-go workplace. This emphasis on practical application to both sports and life in general has led Jackson to focus on methods of consciousness.

Let's apply the seven principles to the Bulls story. The first three terms— *whole*, *essence*, and *potential*—are aspects of the *self* that I am observing and seeking to understand and develop. This self, as we've discovered, can be an individual, a family, a team, a community, or even a nation. And, of course, it can be my own self, which I equally need to understand and develop. I build my capacity for consciousness every time I experience and care about the living beings around me, recognizing the wholeness and potential that are inherent within their selfhood.

Jackson cultivated this aspect of consciousness by helping his players experience *oneness*. In other words, he helped them see themselves as part of a larger self—the team—and reinforced this consciousness through everything from breath exercises to how players learned to read the court. This gave them a basis for experiencing oneness with other wholes: themselves, their fans, the community of professional basketball players they were part of, and, most poignantly, the lives and aspirations of young men in America. By remembering to engage self-to-self with each of these, Jackson's players grew their capacity to be awake, conscious, and able to manage their own inner states, even under extraordinary pressure.

The second three terms—*nestedness*, *nodes*, and *fields*—direct our attention to the *systems* within which a self is embedded and where its potential can be expressed through the contributions it makes. One could say that it is impossible to have a full understanding of the aliveness of something if we can't see it as a self in relation to systems.

Jackson cultivated this aspect of consciousness in his players by encouraging selflessness. Members learned to recognize the simple truth that the collective intelligence and effort of the team could be far more powerful and effective (and inspiring!) than the grandstanding of a single player, no matter how gifted. This became reflected in their after-game interviews, when they spontaneously acknowledged their indebtedness to and appreciation for the efforts of their teammates. And this in turn had a nodal effect on the sport's energy field, presenting an inspiring demonstration of championship basketball carried out in a spirit of courtesy, dignity, mutual respect, and visionary aspiration. Reflecting the influence of his Lakota teachers, Jackson was able to reimagine basketball as a rite of passage for the modern era.

Development, the framework's middle term, serves as a link between the first and second sets of terms, and thus as a link between self and system. Development is a way of seeing and relating to the world. From a developmental perspective, every whole has the capacity to more fully express its essence and potential in the form of new contributions to the systems within which it's nested. Life is not fixed and static; at every level it moves, flows, unfolds, and discovers itself within the movement and unfolding of its context. Each new plateau of expression sets the stage for the next cycle of development, and this is the pulse of evolution.

Phil Jackson expressed profound understanding of the unfolding manifestation of potential in terms of faithfulness. He kept faith with his players by sensing who they could become and encouraging them to develop their potential rather than focusing on the limitations and baggage they arrived with. He kept faith with society by keeping faith with his employers and his sport, always holding up the higher meanings that lay dormant within each. Most important, he kept faith with the spiritual vision that had been shaped by his Pentecostal upbringing and by Lakota and Buddhist teachers. He refers to this vision as the sacred hoop, the inherent oneness in humans and the cosmos.

It wasn't easy to maintain this kind of faith in the high-pressure world of professional sports. It took ongoing effort and considerable inner development, for Jackson and for his teams. After all, they were thinking about and playing basketball in ways that ran directly counter to conventional wisdom and practice. Core to his method was an educational process that continually introduced new, horizon-expanding ideas and practices, starting with oneness, selflessness, and belief that everyone could and should learn how to manage their own state. He required players to put these ideas into practice in the locker room, on the court, and when they socialized together, and he encouraged them to take them home and into the world and practice them there, as well.

This learning process was paired with the use of reflection, such as asking players to reflect on what happened when they allowed themselves to become riled up on the court or about the likely effects of their actions on fans or the young people who saw them as role models. Responsibility and accountability were in the hands of the players. Jackson was careful to avoid telling them what to do or how to behave, which would have undermined the development of their own agency and ability to manage themselves and their environment. The consistent practice of reflection within a high-pressure environment served as an alchemical retort, introducing a purifying fire that enabled players to perform beyond anything they'd imagined was possible. In the process, it allowed the rest of us to witness something astonishing and beautiful, a different way of engaging with life.

SEVENTH INTERMEZZO

Look back to the first intermezzo, where I asked you to list the top five things that you believe about how to make a better world. Then,

- Select two or three of the ideas from the last chapter with which you want to challenge yourself.

- Use them to examine your top five change beliefs, your reflections on them later (second intermezzo), and what you've discovered since.

- Use the first principles to examine what you have tended to miss as you've taken action based on your beliefs.

- Reflect on where and when you fell into the four caveats offered here:

- Socrates Caveat – we mostly see shadows (partial or flawed interpretation of events) and mistake them for reality because we don't examine our minds' faulty working.

- Einstein Caveat – we use old maps and ways of thinking (such as thinking in terms of problem solving); we don't think in new directions so that we can get new outcomes.

- Thomas Kuhn Caveat – we may think we're shifting paradigms, but we aren't able to because we haven't learned to see how the old ones are shaping our thinking.

- David Bohm Caveat – language programs and reenforces our thinking into fragmented images; we are unable to experience living entities as wholes and to discern their essences. What we need to work on is hidden in the effects of this misperception.

Chapter Eight

RESOURCING

I've written this book—and to some extent you've read this book—because we share a sense of urgency about our present moment. Can we change course with regard to the destructive impacts we are having on our planet and become a species that contributes to the richness, diversity, and sheer exuberance with which life evolves and expresses itself in our corner of the universe? Can we regenerate democracy, helping it access the energies it will need to flourish and outgrow the forces currently tearing it apart? Can we invent economies that lift up the human spirit and unleash the creativity that could be our common birthright? Can we restore the sense of the sacred in all of these things, so that our lives are imbued with meaning, purpose, and a sense of belonging?

I care deeply about these questions, and this is why I am also deeply concerned about the ways we are currently pursuing change in our societies. From my point of view, the changes we desperately need are those that can only occur when we've transformed ourselves—our ways of seeing, being, and acting in the world. For this reason, dear reader, it is important to me that the words on these pages are actually intelligible and useful to you. And so I dedicate this closing chapter to a discussion of how the ideas that I've presented can be brought to life and then applied.

Reading Should Be Challenging

In writing this book, I had help from a large group of volunteers who agreed to read the first draft and write about its effect on them. Through their reflections, I was able to gain insight into how the book was working.

The kind of content I'm introducing here doesn't lend itself to our usual ways of reading and processing information. It requires a high degree of investment on the part of readers so that it can be engaged with as something alive, with the power to change their experience of the world. Without this kind of engagement, it becomes a set of abstract intellectual ideas. This was why I created the intermezzos, to shake things up and create at least the possibility of a more awakened engagement with the text.

I learned several important things from my readers about the blind spots that prevented them from fully understanding what I was trying to say. These blind spots are universally present within almost all cultures and seem to be typical of human experience. They are good things to work on in order to grow ourselves. I want to bring them to your attention as something to watch out for and to work on within your own experience.

The first significant blind spot was the failure to see that what I was saying might be new. A number of readers made assumptions about what I believe that were actually untrue. They thought that they agreed with me because they assumed that I would agree with them. In other words, they distorted my meaning in order to fit my ideas into their existing view of the world, experiencing what I'd written as confirmation of what they already believed. Sadly, this prevented them from taking advantage of an opportunity to transform the way that they see the world.

Failing to recognize what is new is a common failure. Even when a reader and author are on more or less the same page, if the reader doesn't use the text to challenge and disrupt the way they think, then the main value the author could deliver is lost. If ideas have depth and power, they can always be used to shake us out of our complacency, but it's up to us to allow them in deeply enough to move and change us.

A second blind spot was readers' failure to recognize the influence their states of being were having on their receptivity to the text. Several readers reported that they were triggered by something in the book that connected to an old story or trauma in their lives. This hindered their ability to actually grasp the point that was being made. Again, this is a common occurrence, one that I am certainly familiar with in my own life. An association with some prior event or conflict causes me to jump track, and I'm no longer present with what's happening in front of me. I have found that learning to manage my state of being is a valuable and necessary aspect of my own development.

A third blind spot consists of deeply ingrained habits with respect to experts and expertise. Those who think of me as an authority would underline passages that they wanted to remember or quote, adding me to the arsenal of expertise that they bring to their work. Those who think of me as a non-expert would reject the ideas I've presented as invalid or inadequately backed up by scientific research. In both cases, readers failed to question themselves in relation to what I presented. This made it difficult for them to speak to these ideas from their own experience and internalized understanding.

A fourth blind spot is, to put it bluntly, lack of humility. I received a number of comments from people who seemed to critique what Phil Jackson and others were actually able to accomplish. These readers appeared to have missed my point entirely. Nowhere in the book do I claim that anyone is perfect or able to achieve perfect results. Perfection is an abstract ideal, not an attribute of living systems.

To criticize the efforts I described as imperfect shows a lack of understanding about what is required for social and systems evolution, which is always indirect, unfinished work in progress. It also betrays an inadequately developed sense of our own personal and professional selves as works in progress. I've noticed that this tendency to criticize those who are willing to risk creative leadership seems to have reached almost epidemic proportions in our present moment. By way of antidote, we might all benefit from a little more humility.

A fifth blind spot is built into our subject of indirect work, which requires us to think about life from outside the mechanistic worldview. This worldview is ubiquitous and entirely invisible to most of us most of the time. To step out of it into what I've characterized as a quantum or David Bohmian worldview means letting go of what we've been taught is self-evidently true about the universe and stepping up to a completely different level of experience. It's a shift that changes everything, from how we understand what's happening around us, to how we think about change, to the meanings and implications of what I've written in these pages. With the intermezzos, I've tried to integrate ways to enable this shift in perception into the reading experience, for I recognize that without it, much of what I've described will seem flat and lifeless.

Becoming a Resource

It may sound as if I'm being harshly judgmental, but let me reassure you that I recognize these patterns because I'm susceptible to them all myself. It seems to me that blind spots are innate in human beings. All of us are deeply conditioned to manifest them, and we all suffer the consequences in the form of limited potential and blocked growth and understanding.

In the tumultuous time in my life when I was newly married and a student at Berkeley, I found myself in over my head. It had finally dawned on me that I didn't know everything and that perhaps I didn't really even know myself. I had always thought that learning was about mastering content—acquiring knowledge and the skills to put it to use. But as a student at Berkeley, I became increasingly aware that I didn't know how to observe and manage my own thinking process, and that this was far more important than the content of my thinking. What I was missing was a method, and fortunately this was what my study of ancient philosophy and Kuhn's theory of paradigm change was beginning to supply.

Since that time, I've organized much of my life and work around the insight that real change comes when we engage consciously with our own mental processes. Along the way, I've become aware of the importance of what I call *resourcing*, which works on awakening in people their capacity for critical thinking and agency with regard to growing and expressing their personal potential. Resourcing is key to how I work on organizational and systems change, and although Phil Jackson wouldn't necessarily have used the word, it's what I see him doing over and over again in the stories he tells in his books.

Resourcing is not mentoring or coaching, both of which assume some kind of superior knowledge. Resourcing is not telling people what to do or guiding them into a better pattern of behavior or performance. Resourcing assumes that the potential to know lies within the individual and that what is needed is to awaken their thirst and discipline to find knowledge within themselves. Put simply, resourcing is fundamentally Socratic.

To be a resource to someone is a profoundly generous and caring act. It requires self-discipline in order to get out of the way of their learning process, allowing it to be nonlinear, indirect, and as destabilizing as it needs to be. Resourcing also requires farsighted and dedicated care for people's *aspirations* and *potential*, and refusal to get hooked by their current strengths, talents, or problems.

In my opinion, we all need resourcing in our lives, and when someone else is not available, we need to know how to resource ourselves. This is where method becomes helpful—for example, one patterned on the approach that Socrates took with his students.

THE SOCRATIC PENTAD

The five blind spots I recognized in my readers' comments became apparent to me because they correlate to a framework titled the Socratic Pentad, which I derived many years ago from my study of the Socratic method. Socrates's approach to the development of free and conscious human beings comprised five disciplines, *aporia, maieutics, elenchus, irony,* and *negating.* Over the years, I have developed personal practices around each of these disciplines as a way to resource myself. I'll share some of them as a way to encourage you to create your own.

THE SOCRATIC PENTAD

Aporia
(Being nonmechanical)

Elenchus
(Using dialog to
examine thinking)

Irony
(Having humility)

Negating
(Ordering worlds and worldviews)

Aporia
(Midwifing self-development)

Aporia refers to the work of waking oneself up. It's probably safe to say that all of us are familiar with absentmindedness, checking out or switching to autopilot, "lights on but nobody home." In this state, our minds and mouths are going through the motions, but very little real thinking is happening. Socrates was acutely aware of this tendency and used unexpected, provocative, confounding questions to disrupt it.

I do the same thing for myself, asking questions that are likely to snap me out of habitual patterns. Sometimes I have to do this in the middle of a situation, when I suddenly become aware that I've gone unconscious. More often, I try to ask myself these questions in advance, when I'm preparing for an interaction, so that my consciousness is engaged from the outset.

One approach is to interrupt myself. I will pull up when I'm roaring down some mental railroad track and ask, "What's going on right now in my mind, with my emotions, and in my body?" This sometimes reveals to me, for example, that I'm experiencing anxiety below the threshold of conscious awareness, and that, unbeknownst to me, it's shaping the way I'm thinking and responding.

Another approach is to notice patterns. Am I using an old, familiar pattern or set of ideas that comes from my past? Am I associating what's happening now with something that happened a long time ago? Is my mind fabricating this connection? Does my choice of words, or the words that I'm emphasizing and repeating, indicate an unconscious attachment on my part? What do I notice about my patterns of behavior? Any one of these can be an indicator that I've fallen asleep; I'm no longer present in the moment and therefore can't shape my responses to be either creative or appropriate.

I encourage you to take a moment while the idea is fresh and create some questions that you can use to wake yourself up. How do you know when you are going through the motions? What can you do to snap yourself out of it? Make some notes so that you can hang on to these questions and keep an eye out for opportunities to put them to use.

Maieutics refers to the work of birthing ourselves, our thoughts, and our consciousness. It derives from the ancient Greek word for midwife and is associated with the Socratic idea of the philosopher as a midwife to the soul. A maieutic process has to do with bringing ideas that are latent, unexamined, or not fully conscious into the light of the mind where they can be tested and evolved to more accurately reflect what is true. At a deeper level, it works on testing and examining ourselves so that we become more accurate reflections of our essence.

I often think of maieutic work as learning to be more capable of managing my own state of being. Every time I allow my thoughts, behaviors, and sense of self to be shaped by unconscious patterns and reactions, I lose connection to that which makes me who I truly am. In those moments, I'm living an unexamined, conditioned life. This is why waking up is so important to me, why I strive to live in present time making conscious, worthy, reality-based choices that might actually make a difference to the situation I'm in. This is almost impossible to do so long as old ghosts are running the show, and so I choose to work on managing myself.

My most reliable maieutic practice is setting an aim for myself by asking, "What is the appropriate state of being for this situation and, therefore, who do I need to consciously work on being?" This enables me to stay awake to what's happening in the moment, while making conscious choices about how I want to respond.

Based on many years of experience, I've also created a set of three aims that provide a more universal pattern for self-management that is grounded in my essence and applies to almost every interaction I find myself in. First, I remind myself to, "Listen actively." This helps me to stay connected with the person or group in front of me and avoid assumptions, preconceptions, or biases with regard to what they are saying.

Second, I tell myself to, "Bring a framework." You've probably noticed that I use frameworks to guide my thinking in all kinds of situations. This is because they help me stay whole and rigorous in my reasoning, and when I can use them explicitly in working with another person, they help us both avoid dropping into conditioned responses. Bringing a framework invites creativity.

Finally, I tell myself, "Seek development." This reminds me to avoid telling people what I think and instead to join with them in generating new thoughts. This benefits both me and them, as it fosters growth and creativity on all sides of the conversation. It also helps sidestep conflict and move us toward shared understanding.

Over the years, I've found that the ability to set an aim has been critical to strengthening my capability to manage my state and that it works well, even when I'm faced with high-pressure situations. I invite you to give it a try, right now. What state of being would you like to aim for as you continue reading this chapter? How can you essentialize this thought into a couple of words that are positive, proactive, and easy to remember and put to use?

Elenchus introduces the idea of rigor and discipline into our work as resources. An elenctic process helps us to develop the ability to test and challenge the ideas we encounter in the world, overcoming the tendency to simply adopt them out of mental laziness. Whenever I borrow ideas without testing them in my own experience, I'm guilty of this kind of laziness. It doesn't matter whether these ideas came from someone else or I generated them myself in the past; if I accept them as established and true, then I've abdicated responsibility for deepening my own thinking.

At first this may sound a little extreme. I can imagine many people wondering how we would ever progress in our lives or as societies if we couldn't accept the things that we've proven to ourselves as established and certain and move on from there. The problem arises from generalizing our experiences, as though specific cases provided a basis for drawing general conclusions.

I'm proposing a very different approach, which is to treat each new situation, each new moment, each new person, group, community, or ecosystem, as unique, unpredictable, and imbued with its own potential, to be discovered and manifested. This requires having the mental discipline to start fresh, creating new ideas from the materials at hand in the moment. It's a high standard to hold oneself to, but I can report—from my own experience and what I've heard from many other people—that with exercise it becomes a natural mode of thought and being. You get good at it, and life becomes richer and more compelling, dynamic, and meaningful as a result.

I mentioned above that I always try to bring a framework into my thinking. This is my way of engaging an elenctic practice in work and life. Used correctly, frameworks demand rigor, wholeness, and fresh thinking; in this regard, they are very different from mental models, which evoke a repetitive or formulaic approach.

Perhaps the Socratic Pentad that we are currently exploring provides a demonstration of this. The framework doesn't tell me *what* to think, but it gives me a potent method for understanding and upgrading the *way* that I'm thinking. It only works if I'm honest and real about what's happening in my mind right now, if I take it *personally* and apply it in the moment to this particular situation. The Socratic method loses its power if I allow it to become abstract or intellectual.

Frameworks enable us to reframe, to break up the unconscious structures or patterns of our thoughts. Framework thinking is a deep discipline that requires years to master. It's a bit like learning a new language, but anyone can learn to apply specific frameworks to help them reframe.

This book, like all of my books, offers a number of frameworks as ways to break up conventional or habitual ways of seeing things in order to shed new light on them. I encourage you to go back and use these frameworks, finding places where they apply to your life or what you are working on. Can you find one to apply right now, as you continue reading this book? What does the intention to use a framework add to your reading experience? If you are a person who really wants to make change in the world, you are likely to discover that this practice can be both exciting and liberating because of the ways that frameworks disrupt old habits of thinking and perception.

Irony, in its Socratic sense, flows naturally from having willingly given up certainty. As I see it, Socrates wasn't mocking or playing a trick on his interlocutors when he professed ignorance of the subjects they were exploring together. Rather, he used irony to prevent them from looking to him for answers. By adopting the role of learner seeking to be enlightened, he joined with his students in a process of discovery that required them to stand on their own feet, developing their own understanding. He was demonstrating the practice and discipline of bringing himself to every subject anew. This required humility on his part and a willingness to publicly acknowledge his limitations, even to the point of making himself, the lover of wisdom, appear as a buffoon—the visual and visceral image of not knowing. It also opened up an ability to truly be with his students, using the ferocious power of his intellect and wisdom in service to their own self-discovery.

This kind of irony is an ongoing, and very challenging, part of my practice. You could say that it is a source of suffering that I've had to willingly embrace in order to become a resource to the many people I wish to serve. Throughout my childhood I had been told by an abusive father that I was an ignorant girl who would never amount to anything. I fought hard for my intellectual accomplishments, and they have always served to demonstrate to me and others that what my father said was untrue. It isn't easy for me to publicly deny my knowledge and adopt a stance of ignorance. Yet to do so is both true and necessary—true because I am a learner who is committed to undermining my own certainties and necessary because this is the way I engage in the indirect work of building self-accountability and self-determination in society.

The irony practice that I use has an inner dimension. I begin by challenging myself to look beyond what I believe I know in order to seek out gaps in my understanding, where my thinking needs to be undermined and then evolved. The practice also has an outer dimension; I consistently remind people that I am not an expert, that I am a work in progress, here to learn something together with them. The good news is that this is often disarming. Instead of spending a lot of energy trying to demonstrate to me how smart they are and why my ideas are wrong, people are likely as not to join with me to come up with new ideas.

As with each of the other practices I've described, I encourage you to try this out for yourself, sooner rather than later. Ask yourself, "What is it about me that I would rather not admit, to myself or anyone else? What would I prefer that no one find out about me?" Invite yourself to look at this quality, acknowledging and accepting that it is there, and explore its implications and consequences in your life and work. Then think about a way to expose this aspect of yourself in a more public way.

If this feels really difficult or risky, try doing it in a relatively safe environment, building some ironic muscle before taking on broader public exposure. The point isn't to embarrass yourself, although a bit of embarrassment is probably good for the development of humility. The point is to overcome the tyrannical tendencies of a top-down, expert-worshipping culture, inviting honest engagement and collaboration among people who are learning to think of themselves as co-learners.

Negating, the discipline that gives the Socratic method its depth, is basically about being dissatisfied with the surfaces of things. Whenever we become generic or superficial in our thinking, negating demands that we go deeper, asking ourselves, "What is at the core of this subject; what is its essence? Why is it profoundly important to me and to life in general?" We learn to reject anything that is facile, lacking in nuance, complexity, and indeterminacy.

In my case, I have adopted a three-part practice to help go deeper with the things I'm working on. First of all, I place a demand on myself to never do anything the same way twice. I made this promise more than 40 years ago, and it has served me well in terms of developing my creativity and elevating my thinking. It has also served my clients and students, who have come to expect the unexpected from me.

Second, I make everything specific and relevant. I always test my ideas and designs with regard to how they will affect a particular person or situation, now, in the present moment. I avoid generic ideas like the plague, and I avoid recycling old speeches or workshop designs as though they could be shoehorned into new situations for which they were never intended. Keeping my attention on real people who are living and working in real contexts is great for making my understanding alive, fresh, and relevant to how the world works.

Third, I deepen the relevance of what I'm doing by deepening my understanding of who I'm doing it for. That is, I seek to take into account their essence, potential, and core motivations, and the contributions they aspire to make with their lives. In other words, I apply the first principles of living systems to the individuals and groups I work with so that I can engage them from a conscious level.

I have a suggestion for building a practice like this for oneself. Create a simple ritual, something that I call a *stop exercise*. Think of an activity that has become fairly routine but would benefit from increased creativity and higher-level thinking, such as teaching a class, correcting a child, or giving a slideshow presentation. As you begin work on this activity, stop yourself and ask, "What am I doing that I've done before? How could I make it new and more relevant for this person or audience? Who are they really, and what really is the essence of what I'm trying to communicate?" You can find the right questions for yourself, so long as you remember to stop the impulse to go on automatic.

RESOURCING ONESELF

The intermezzos that weave through this book represent a kind of writing experiment. I wanted to find a way to evoke conscious participation and critical thinking rather than passive information consumption. I wanted to see if it was possible for an author to be a resource to you, the reader, inviting you to observe and evolve your own reading process as you moved through the text.

At the same time, I wanted to make all of this explicit, as clear and direct as possible, because once you set the book down, the author is no longer able to serve the role of resource. If this engagement has seeded a sense of excitement in you, a sense that there's something here that you want to pursue, then it becomes imperative that you be able to resource yourself.

The frameworks and ideas offered here describe a way of thinking about systems change, but to use them requires that we each be doing our own inner work. The Socratic Pentad, as useful as it is for engaging others, is also a powerful instrument for working on oneself. For example, it was continuously present as part of my own process in writing this book. My aim was to bring something into the world that reflected, to the best of my ability, integrity between the content and the way it was created. So it was important to wake myself up, manage my state, challenge my own thinking, cultivate a bit of humility, and, wherever possible, deepen and evolve my understanding of what I was trying to communicate.

It is through internalizing a framework that one earns the right to bring it into work with others. It's in this spirit that I invite you to internalize the Socratic Pentad in order to resource yourself. In this way, you become a better resource for all those around you who would benefit from your goodwill and desire to make a contribution to the world. The work is indirect, based on growing our collective capacity for understanding, and it can begin right here, right now, with how you grow your own.

EIGHTH INTERMEZZO

Review and reflect on all of the writing you have done for the intermezzos. Use the Socratic Pentad to examine your process at a new level of rigor.

- Which thoughts do you seem attached to without any reasonable justification? You will be able to distinguish these because you have generated energy around them that is infused with emotion (e.g., defensiveness, upset, joy, comfort). How might you examine these further in order to develop an aporetic process? Do this examining now or schedule a time in the near future when you can work on it.

- Where do your reflections seem to indicate a need to *birth a new version of yourself?* Where can you see in retrospect that personal growth may be called for? This may be something you have observed before that has now become obvious and perhaps uncomfortable. You might feel the urge to move it to a front burner. Design a maieutic process based on your reflections on the pentad and prepare to engage in it.

- As you read the book, where did you find yourself readily accepting or rejecting my ideas? Unless you have since examined them to trace their source and test their rigor, these will have become borrowed ideas. Design an elenctic process to face up to these surprising or expected observations and prepare to engage in it.

- Where did you observe your hubris arising and coming into play? You think you know more than me, Phil Jackson, or even Socrates. You have done what we do better and gotten better outcomes. Or, at the very least, you can critique the processes we used or the outcomes and effects they achieved. Design an ironic process and prepare to engage in it.

- Where do you see the shallowness and laziness of your thinking? You may notice yourself speaking in platitudes or rehearsing pat thoughts you've been carrying around for years. You may frequently latch onto explanations and rationales based on previous events and memorized ways of expressing them. Design a negating process to evolve yourself and prepare to engage in it.

- Finally, step back and look at the Socratic Pentad as a whole. Try drawing it in your journal, adding a word or phrase beneath each ancient Greek word to help you evoke the process it names. As the different processes shed light on one another, see if you can experience the questions you just answered as a continuous flow of work. The framework will be most useful when it becomes alive to you and you are able to practice the disciplines that it describes as aspects of a dynamic whole.

AFTERWORD

DEVELOPMENTAL COMMUNITIES

Resourcing oneself is powerful and necessary work, but it's also hard to do. After all, we humans have a tendency to avoid the extra effort involved. We take short-cuts, forget to follow through, lessen the rigor of our processes, and, before long, find ourselves back where we started. This is why I believe that one of the most important reasons for human social exchange is that we need the friction, chal-lenge, and encouragement of other people to grow ourselves.

Because of this, I've spent most of my adult life participating in, and at times stewarding, communities that are dedicated above all to the conscious develop-ment of their members. In such communities, we resource one another, always with the aim of building a field within which consciousness can grow and deepen.

Whether you seek to apply indirect work to an organization, as Phil Jackson did with the Chicago Bulls, or a social change movement, or a town that wants better lives for its citizens, you will benefit greatly from doing so as a member of a developmental community. Developing ourselves is a lifelong effort, and it is hard to sustain force without the challenge and nurturance provided by a community of like-minded seekers.

In my experience, there are several key qualities that distinguish a *developmental* community from support groups, social circles, professional associations, houses of worship, and other places we rely on for human connection. The first of these qualities is an explicit and transparent agreement to share a developmental method, such as Socrates's, as opposed to a dogma or rules of behavior. This enables everyone to be self-accountable for the work that they do in the group, which makes the community democratic in the best sense: each member is becoming better and better at governing themself. Also, by making the method transparent, everyone has the opportunity to upgrade their application of its practices and, ultimately, to evolve them.

The second key quality is a certain level of structure that allows the group to gather on a regular, recurring basis to engage in thoughtfully designed developmental processes. A regularly recurring pattern is important because it builds the ability to sustain growth over time. People are able to connect the dots between what they learned in one session and what they will learn in the next, and this allows them to progress as individuals, deepening both their capability and capacity. As the years pass, the group, too, will progress, taking on challenges of increasing complexity and significance. Also, being in a familiar setting with familiar people creates a shared energy field, and this reinforces the quality of intention and dedicated effort necessary to generate the value that the group is seeking for its members.

The third key quality is a shared epistemology based on the idea that people only come to a transformational understanding of themselves and reality when they take responsibility for their own development. People are immersed in an environment where the demand for self-development is ubiquitous, and one that includes older, more established participants alongside those who are stepping onto the path for the first time. The process uses concrete events in people's own lives as the raw material for their self-inquiry. This is important because the transformational potential of the work is lost the minute an epistemology of self-development drops out and an epistemology of expertise and greater knowledge steps in to replace it.

Finally, I believe that the people in such a community need to view one another as friends, not in a social sense, but in the sense of being unshakably (and at times ruthlessly) committed to one another's growth and development. These *friends in the work* don't seek ease or comfort in their relationships with one another, but rather to challenge and lift one another up to live out the aspirations that each holds for a meaningful life. This is important because we humans love our comfort, and we frequently seek out people who make us feel comfortable. Having friends in the work can serve as a refreshing antidote to this sleepy habit, a place in our lives where we've specifically chosen to be among people who have agreed to challenge us.

Of course, people being people, whenever we are in a group that is dedicated to some mutual effort, we will inevitably find that some members rub us the wrong way. When the group commitment is to consciousness, this irritant becomes a rich opportunity for waking up and getting over ourselves. Also, having a shared developmental commitment helps rein in the tendency to allow more conventional social interactions, such as gossip or small talk, to bleed off the energy and focus of the group.

Existing Developmental Communities

I believe that there is real value in working to create developmental groups wherever you are. I also recognize that it may not be easy to find people who share your motivation or who have the skill to pull off what is, really, a very demanding practice. For this reason, I'm also including here a web address for the various developmental communities that I design and steward. Because these communities meet online and are found in different parts of the world, it is possible to join one from pretty much anywhere.

https:\\seed-communities.com

Because I am committed to helping people become accountable for their own development, I always impose certain restraints to joining one of these communities. I want you to be really clear that this is the right place for you and that you are willing to do the work that it takes to be a contributing member. This is all explained in detail on the web page. If this sounds appealing to you, I invite you to visit the SEED Communities website to see if it might be a good fit.

Appreciation and Indebtedness

First and foremost, I want to express my appreciation for my longtime co-creative partner in producing books and papers. For me, Ben Haggard is a developmental editor who makes sure that ideas are well-structured, compelling, and enticingly presented; that they flow well and make sense; that the arc of the book rises and falls as it should through each paragraph and chapter; and that it captures what I really want to say, often in language that goes beyond what I believed myself capable of. Ben walks with me from chapter to chapter, pushing me to be inventive and insightful. No redundancy, sloppiness, or confusion are allowed. I would not be an author without him, much less here with book number six.

Kit Brewer, another core member of our team, is a taskmaster to both of us, demanding precision and rigor in word choice and order. She champions the reader, making sure to the best of her ability that they will grasp both the meaning and the spirit of the text and, with luck, be pulled into it with joy. Plus, she hunts down stray commas, fanciful spellings, faulty word choice, and improvisational grammar like the copy editor from hell, teaching us as she goes.

I also want to thank my beta readers, 30 in total, for their willingness to undertake the demanding regime I asked of them. Each of them did a set of exercises (included here as intermezzos following chapters) that challenged them to consciously observe their experience as they read, and they kept journals of their reflections, which they summarized for me. I asked them specifically to share reflections on themselves as readers rather than to make direct suggestions for improving the content. These reflections enabled me to *see* how people engaged with the book, providing a reliable picture of what was likely to happen when other readers encountered it, and this helped me assess and fine-tune my approach. As an added benefit, more than half of my readers reported that they learned things about themselves from the intermezzos and would never read a book the same way again.

One beta reader to whom I am particularly indebted is Michiel Bakker, Vice President of Global Workplace Services Programs at Google, my friend in the work. He read the book more than once and helped me to see what I was missing—or, more accurately, what I was not helping my readers to see with regard to what I was intending to convey. Our conversations led to a great deal of rewriting, augmenting, and illustrating that I trust have made the book easier to grasp and put to use.

The team at Book Launchers—Julie Broad, Jaqueline Kyle, and Sarah Bean—do the real work of getting my self-published books into the world. They've managed production from cover design, to printing, to e-book formatting, to marketing. But more than this, they have been friends and allies, even helping to revert the rights to my first two books back to me so that I could republish them in a new edition. I am unapologetically enthusiastic about publishing with this amazing team and would not choose to work with anyone else.

And to all the members of The Regenerative Communities (change agents, women entrepreneurs, educators, and business teams), for which I design materials and steward global developmental events. They teach me by their excellent personal, professional, and business development work, and I gain hope and faith in our collective future as I see them grow and contribute in the world. It is inspiring and instructive to be in their presence.